East Meets Southwest

NATURAL FUSION CUISINE

Lynn Walters

THE CROSSING PRESS
FREEDOM, CALIFORNIA

Acknowledgments

I am very grateful to Barbara Feller-Roth, my editor, for encouragement, patience, and clarity throughout the writing of this book.

For feeding me well and teaching me that cooking is a creative and important part of life, I thank my mother, Ruth Walters, who tested many recipes for this book even as she went about her busy life, sewing magnificent quilts and running a business. I am grateful to my father, Stanley Walters, who taught me to appreciate good food and integrity. I dedicate this book to my parents.

My great appreciation goes to Judy Knapp and Marion Carter for testing and revising recipes, reading the manuscript, and offering many helpful suggestions. Thanks also to Martha Flannery, Charles Owen, and Michael Gintert.

I particularly wish to thank the diligent people who tested recipes for this book—family and friends Larry Merica, Martha Henderson, Peggy Wright, Mary Bernheim, Jean Hofstra, Katie Sward, Sandra Pope, Bobby Knapp, and Sarah Jewler.

To Willis Rayl goes my lifelong appreciation for encouraging me to be myself.

My love to my son, Peer, my daughter, Lily, and special appreciation to my husband, Peter, for his unwavering encouragement, patience, and love of simple pleasures. Appreciation and love to my sister Robyn Barst, a woman of myriad talents.

I am most grateful to Shrikrishna Kashyap, my friend and teacher, who has lighted the way so many times, and who reminds me that we must all thank God for the bounty of this earth and the richness of our lives.

Library of Congress Cataloging-in-Publication Data

Walters, Lynn (Lynn Marie)
    East meets Southwest : natural fusion cuisine / by Lynn Walters.
        p.cm
    Rev. ed. of: Cooking at the Natural Cafe in Santa Fe. c1992.
    ISBN 1-58091-086-6 (pbk)
    1. Cookery (Natural foods) 2. Natural Cafe (Santa Fe, N.M.) I.Walters, Lynn (Lynn Marie) Cooking at the Natural Cafe in Santa Fe. II. Title

TX741.W35 2000
  641.5'63--dc21   00-030711

Contents

Introduction

My grandmother was a wild cook. She often just threw together meals that were fantastic. My mother recently told me that, when my grandmother occasionally used a cookbook, she often, unwittingly, read from two recipes on the same page, combining ingredients and methods. Although this is not a procedure I recommend, she must have had incredible intuition and good taste, because her meals were always delicious.

I may have inherited some of her ways, for I have never liked the confines of recipes. However, I have learned to appreciate them for guidance and new ideas. Running a restaurant has taught me the value of consistency, which either an intelligent mind or a well-written recipe can provide. At The Natural Cafe, new cooks must learn how to decipher my chicken scratches on our recipes, but more importantly, how to taste, and when and how to improvise.

Cooking begins with love, which is the thread of life. The foods that we gather and prepare nourish our bodies and spirits as they maintain our life-sustaining link to the earth. The act of cooking, like any act of love, transforms the individual as well as the food.

As a working mother, I have felt the temptation of "convenience" foods, but so far, my love of flavor and good health, as well as the knowledge that cooking doesn't have to take the entire day, has saved me from the frozen food section of the supermarket. I encourage you to eat freshly made food whenever possible; to trust your intuition and ability to prepare delicious food quickly and easily "from scratch."

Preparing good food requires both intuition and rational thought. The five senses—sight, smell, taste, touch, and hearing—all contribute to this process. Through the senses you experience the results of varied methods of cooking—for example, the differences between boiling, baking, and sautéing an onion. Although the raw ingredient is the same, the color, fragrance, flavor, and texture will change with each method. Though we generally don't think of sound as a key to cooking, it can be an important indicator. If you sprinkle a drop of water on a pan, the sound of the sizzle can tell you how hot the pan is. As you learn from observation, you will develop the confidence to create many wonderful meals.

Cookbooks offer recipes and inspiration. My wish for this one is that it will encourage you to explore and experience the unique relationships between you, the food, and the fire. Learning to cook is an evolution with no end. And then there is the eating….

Ingredients

Find the best ingredients. This does not necessarily mean the most expensive, but often those foods that are grown closest to your home and that are in season. In our world of fast travel and shipping, this old idea of using locally grown foods is once again being appreciated.

If you are fortunate enough to have a small plot of land, you may discover the pleasure of eating the freshest fruits and vegetables possible, combined with the privilege of seeing how they grow. It is a great joy for me to grow food. I have the feel and smell of the earth in spring and the excitement of watching seedlings emerge from their sleep. And nothing can compare to running through ten-foot-tall purple corn!

We garden organically and purchase organic foods whenever possible. The fact remains that "organic" just means grown naturally, without chemicals, and that healthy food can be elegant and delicious. In our technological egoism, we sometimes forget that nature's ways are beautiful and that they work exceedingly well.

Recipe format: The recipes in this book list each ingredient in order, each time it is used. This means that an ingredient may be listed more than once. We have found this to be an efficient method, which we trust you will find helpful, too.

Seasoning

A dear friend has been teaching and teasing me about salt for many years. When we met, I was reacting to the overuse of salt in many foods by using very little, believing that the true flavor of the food would triumph. This is not always true. Salt has wonderful properties if used appropriately. It enhances flavors by bringing them to their peak. Salt is also a great preserver of flavor, texture, and color. Do not be afraid of salt, but use it with discrimination. I recommend natural sea salt.

Classic seasonings have been time tested, but do experiment. Beware, however, of combining foods or seasonings just for the sake of variety. When I began cooking professionally, I would take out many jars of herbs and spices and smell their fragrances, imagining how each would mingle with the flavors of the dish that was cooking. It was an enlightening experience! When I found a pleasing combination, I would take a pinch of that herb or spice and add it to a spoonful from the cooking pot. Tasting these experiments provided experience without the risk of ruining an entire meal. With increased sensitivity you can learn to season from aroma alone.

Fresh herbs can be a revelation. When I first tasted fresh basil, I hardly recognized it. Compared with dried basil, it had so much more fragrance and a hint of cinnamon that mingled with the deeper, more familiar flavor. Other fresh herbs will surprise and delight your palate. If you have any desire to garden, experiment with herbs. They merely need a sunny spot outside or a bright window-sill, and a caring, yet casual, hand.

To stock your pantry with dried herbs, purchase them frequently in small quantities. By doing this you will be assured of the best flavor when you season your food.

Whenever possible, use freshly squeezed juices (for example, lemon juice) in cooking. They have more flavor and vitamins when fresh.

To make ginger juice, finely grate fresh ginger, then squeeze the grated ginger in your hand to extract the juice. You may also squeeze the grated ginger through a garlic press, kept especially for this purpose.

Black pepper is a wonderful spice that I took for granted for many years. Grinding fresh pepper in a peppermill is easy, and the flavor is worlds away from commercially ground pepper. If you need a large quantity or desire especially coarsely ground pepper, grind whole peppercorns in a spice mill or a blender. To grind the pepper in a blender, pulse on high speed.

Myriad varieties of fresh and dried chiles are available. I primarily use Chimayo red chile, New Mexico red and green chiles, and anaheim and jalapeño chiles. Chimayo red chile is a flavorful medium-hot chile that can be obtained either as whole dried chiles or ground into a coarse brick-red powder.

In this book, when ground red chile is called for, please use ground Chimayo or New Mexico red chile if possible. If you are unable to find these chiles in a gourmet grocery, purchase ground ancho chile. Do not use chili powder, which is a blend of cayenne pepper, cumin, oregano, and other spices.

The crushed red chile called for in these recipes is usually made from the chile piquin, a small fiery red chile. It is widely available in most grocery stores and is sometimes known as red pepper flakes.

A Few Notes on Cookware

I use stainless steel and cast iron cooking pans, and enameled cast iron. I remember once cooking some rhubarb in an aluminum pan and being amazed at how clean and shiny the pan became. It didn't occur to me at the time that we were eating the layer of aluminum that was missing. Aluminum has been implicated as the cause of some debilitating diseases. If you must use aluminum pans occasionally, be sure that you are cooking nonacid foods.

Stainless steel is not completely nonreactive, but it is quite stable. Cast iron does give some iron to the food cooked in it, which is good for most of us. Unchipped enameled pans are neutral, relatively nonstick, and generally a joy to use.

I encourage you to purchase a few high-quality utensils and pans rather than many poor-quality ones. A small selection of saucepans is useful: one small (1 quart), one or two medium (2 quarts), one large (4 quarts), and possibly a larger stockpot for soups and pasta. A pressure cooker is helpful for cooking beans and grains, especially if you live at a high altitude. A stainless steel colander is useful for rinsing vegetables and draining pasta.

Knives are important, their sharpness being paramount. High-carbon stainless steel knives are easy to keep clean and stay sharp longer than less expensive stainless steel knives. Regular steel rusts easily but will stay sharp the longest. I recommend either sharpening your knives regularly or finding someone trustworthy to do it for you.

For baking, it is nice to have at least two small bowls (1 quart), one or two medium bowls (1 1/2 quarts), and one large bowl (2 quarts). If you bake bread, you may want an extra-large bowl as well. I prefer ceramic or glass bowls, but stainless steel also works well.

A few wooden spoons and a wire whisk are needed for mixing. It is useful to have a good set of stainless steel measuring spoons, a set of stainless steel measuring cups (for dry ingredients), and a glass measuring cup (for liquids).

There are many kitchen gadgets available. Have fun with them, but remember that simple cookware is all you need. To work in a clean, uncluttered kitchen is a pleasure.

Soups

In olden days soups were a mainstay, simmering on the stove, warm and fragrant. Today they often seem to be viewed as humble beginnings that don't really count.

To me, soups exemplify the simple alchemy of cooking. Separate herbs, vegetables, legumes, and fruits combine to become much more than the sum of the ingredients. This transformation is wondrous.

These recipes are all quite easy, though some may take more time to prepare than others. All of these soups are good prepared according to the recipes, but after making them once, please try your own alterations and variations. Realizing the myriad of choices in cooking opens up many possibilities. Changing your cutting, cooking, heat, and time results in bright or muted colors, crisp or tender texture, and direct or complex flavors. Think about why warming winter soups often need long and slow cooking, whereas a chilled summer soup may need none.

Bean soups may be made with just water for liquid, although the addition of a simple stock enriches them. Most of the vegetable soups, however, really need stock or they are apt to taste watery. The vegetable stock recipe presented here is very simple, but it does take some planning. If you absolutely do not have the time, substitute a dehydrated vegetable broth.

Immediately before serving a soup, taste it to adjust the seasoning, and thin it if necessary with stock, water, or cream, depending on the soup.

Two tips on serving: In cold weather, warm the soup bowls on the stove, in the oven, or with hot water; and always prepare a garnish that is beautiful and complementary in flavor. Serving is an art that need not be confined to trained chefs.

Simple Vegetable Stock

▼▼▼▼▼▼▼▼▼▼▼▼▼

Slowly simmered vegetables transform pure water into a delicately flavored stock that can provide an important background for the main ingredients of any soup or sauce. It is most important in purely vegetable soups; bean soups are enhanced by stock, but are possible to make with only water.

This recipe is for an all-purpose vegetable stock, but please feel free to vary the ingredients to suit your taste and the requirements of the dish you are going to prepare.

2 green onions, washed and cut into 2-inch pieces
1 medium yellow or white onion, peeled and sliced
1 stalk celery, cut into large pieces
1 carrot, cut into large pieces
1/4 cup chopped, washed parsley, stems included
2 cabbage leaves or 1 broccoli stalk (not the florets)
1 piece (1 to 2 inches) kombu seaweed, optional (see Note)
10 cups cool water

Place all the ingredients in a large saucepan or pressure cooker. Bring to a boil and simmer for 1 to 3 hours, or pressure cook for 1 hour.

Strain the stock through a fine sieve, reserving the kombu if desired. The other vegetables have given up their essence, and should be discarded or composted.

Use the stock immediately, or if keeping for more than a few hours, add salt to taste and keep covered in the refrigerator for up to 2 days. (The salt will preserve the stock at this point; adding it earlier would inhibit the vegetables from releasing their full flavor into the stock.)

Makes 6 to 8 cups.

Note: Kombu adds flavor and minerals to the stock. It may be found at natural foods markets and Asian grocery stores.

Martha's Carrot Soup

▼▼▼▼▼▼▼▼▼▼▼▼▼

Martha Flannery, a dear friend, baker, seamstress, and soother of savage beasts, made this soup famous. It is a delicious and, most often, nondairy delight. This soup is easy to prepare. Its success depends on richly flavored stock, sweet carrots, and carmelized onions. Taste your carrots before you begin.

2 pounds carrots, peeled, trimmed, and cut into 2-inch pieces
7 cups Simple Vegetable Stock (see page 10)
1 medium yellow onion, sliced or diced
1 tablespoon corn oil or unsalted butter
1/4 teaspoon white pepper
3/4 teaspoon salt, or to taste
1/2 to 1 teaspoon ginger juice, optional (see page 7)
1 teaspoon minced parsley, for garnish

Place the carrots in a large saucepan and cover with the vegetable stock. Bring to a boil, then simmer until the carrots are very tender.

Meanwhile, over high heat, saute the onion in the corn oil until golden brown. Reduce the heat and continue to cook until the onion becomes very soft and caramelized.

Pour the carrots and enough stock to cover them into a blender container. Blend until smooth. Pour the remaining stock over the caramelized onion. Pour the blended carrots back into the large saucepan.

Blend the onion and stock as you blended the carrots. Add this mixture to the carrot mixture and cook over low heat until hot but not boiling, approximately 5 minutes. Add the white pepper, salt, and ginger juice, if desired. Taste for seasonings. Serve garnished with the minced parsley.

This soup is best served the day it is made because it loses its wonderful sweetness quickly. It may be kept, covered in the refrigerator, for 1 day.

Serves 4 to 6.

Variation: An Afghani cook brought us this spicy version: Add 1/2 to 1 hot green chile (jalapeño), seeded and minced, to the caramelized onion and sauté until bright green. Stir 1 tablespoon minced cilantro into the finished soup. Use cilantro leaves for garnish.

Chile Corn Chowder

▼▼▼▼▼▼▼▼▼▼▼▼▼▼▼▼

It is time to make this soup when the fields of grain are turning golden and the sweet corn is ripe in your garden or at a roadside stand down the road. This chowder takes more preparation than one made from frozen corn kernels, but to me the added flavor is worth the time. If you substitute frozen corn, you may want to add more seasoning.

3 large white potatoes or 5 small potatoes
Water, to cover potatoes
1 large yellow or white onion, finely diced
1 1/2 tablespoons unsalted butter
1/4 teaspoon salt
1 carrot, peeled and diced into 1/4-inch cubes
1 mild green chile (anaheim), seeded and finely diced
1/4 teaspoon black pepper
1/2 cup lightly roasted yellow cornmeal (see Note)
1 1/2 cups Simple Vegetable Stock (see page 10)
3 cups Simple Vegetable Stock (see page 10)
Kernels from 5 ears sweet corn (approximately 2 cups)
1/4 cup finely diced celery
1 1/2 cups whipping cream
1 cup milk
2 tablespoons minced parsley
1/2 teaspoon minced fresh marjoram
or 1/4 teaspoon dried marjoram
Pinch cayenne pepper, optional
3/4 teaspoon salt, or to taste
2 tablespoons minced red bell pepper, for garnish

Cover the potatoes with water in a medium saucepan and cook over high heat until the water boils. Reduce the heat and simmer until the potatoes are just tender when pierced with a knife or a wooden skewer. Let cool in cold water, then peel, dice into 1/2-inch cubes, and reserve.

In a large saucepan over medium-high heat, sauté the onion in the butter with the 1/4 teaspoon salt until sweet and golden brown. Add the carrot, chile, and black pepper. Cook only until the chile is bright green and lightly browned.

In a small bowl whisk together the roasted cornmeal and the 1 1/2 cups stock. Add this mixture, the reserved potatoes, and the 3 cups stock to the sautéed vegetables. Simmer over low heat until the soup begins to thicken, 20 to 30 minutes, stirring occasionally.

Add the corn and celery and simmer only until the corn is tender and the celery is bright green and slightly crunchy, 5 to 10 minutes.

Add the cream, milk, seasonings, and the 3/4 teaspoon salt. Taste for salt and pepper and heat until steaming. Do not boil.

Garnish with the red bell pepper and serve immediately. This soup will keep, covered in the refrigerator, for 1 to 2 days.

Serves 6 to 8.

Note: Although roasting the cornmeal is not absolutely necessary, it sweetens and deepens the flavor. To roast: In a small, heavy-bottomed saucepan, dry-roast the cornmeal over medium heat until fragrant but not browned. Immediately pour the cornmeal into a bowl to cool.

Cream of Mushroom Soup
▼▼▼▼▼▼▼▼▼▼▼▼▼

My mother has always been a very good cook, but one thing she never made "from scratch" was cream of mushroom soup. This recipe was actually inspired by my fond memories of the canned cream of mushroom soup that my mother often served us. This feels like an embarrassing confession to make, but it is the truth.

1 medium white or yellow onion, finely diced
1 tablespoon unsalted butter
1/4 teaspoon salt
1 pound mushrooms, sliced
2 teaspoons soy sauce
1/4 to 1/2 teaspoon black pepper, to taste
1/4 cup unsalted butter
1/2 cup unbleached white flour
3 cups Simple Vegetable Stock (see page 10)
1 stalk celery, finely diced
1/4 teaspoon dried oregano
1/4 teaspoon dried rosemary
1/8 teaspoon dried thyme
Pinch cayenne pepper
1/4 to 1/2 teaspoon salt, to taste
1/3 cup whipping cream
3/4 cup half-and-half or whole milk
2 tablespoons minced parsley

In a large saucepan over medium-high heat, sauté the diced onion in the 1 tablespoon butter. When hot add the 1/4 teaspoon salt. Cook, stirring frequently, until the onion is golden and sweet.

Add the sliced mushrooms, soy sauce, and black pepper, and saute until the liquid from the mushrooms is gone and the mushrooms are seared to a medium brown.

Meanwhile, make the roux. In a medium saucepan melt the 1/4 cup butter. Add the flour and cook until the flour smells toasty but is not browned, 1 to 3 minutes. Remove from the heat and slowly whisk in 1 cup of the vegetable stock. Continue adding the stock, whisking constantly, until all 3 cups are incorporated and there are no lumps.

Add the stock mixture to the mushrooms and simmer over low heat for 5 minutes. Add the diced celery, dried herbs, and cayenne and simmer until the celery is tender, 10 to 15 minutes longer.

Add the salt to taste, cream, and half-and-half, and heat but do not boil. Taste for salt and other seasonings. Stir in the parsley and serve.

This soup will keep refrigerated for up to 2 days, but it will need additional salt and pepper.

Serves 4 to 6.

<u>Variation:</u> Instead of using oregano and rosemary, substitute 1 1/2 teaspoons fresh tarragon or 1/2 teaspoon dried tarragon.

Beet Soup

▼▼▼▼▼▼▼▼▼▼▼▼▼▼▼

Although I occasionally like to make a more traditional borscht, this simply blended version is beautiful and tasty. The key is the flavor of the beets. You may choose to make this soup with golden beets. In that case, cook a carrot with the beets to enhance the color, and garnish the soup with grated red beets.

2 pounds beets, trimmed
Water, to cover beets
1 medium white or yellow onion, sliced or diced
1 tablespoon corn or other light vegetable oil
1/4 teaspoon salt
7 cups Simple Vegetable Stock (see page 10)
1/4 teaspoon white pepper
3/4 teaspoon salt, or to taste
1/3 cup sour cream, optional garnish
1 teaspoon minced parsley, for garnish

Place the beets in a large saucepan, cover with water, and bring to a rolling boil. Reduce the heat so that the liquid is simmering and cook until the beets are very soft but not falling apart, 45 minutes to 1 hour. Drain the beets (see Note) and cover with cold water.

Meanwhile, sauté the onion in the oil with the 1/4 teaspoon salt. Cook over medium-high heat until the onion is golden brown and very sweet, almost caramelized.

Drain the beets again, and again cover with cold water. Now proceed to peel the beets; the skins should slip off easily. If they do not, the beets probably need further cooking. Place half the peeled beets in a blender container with half the cooked onion and half the stock. Blend until smooth. Pour the blended soup into a large saucepan. Blend the other half of the cooked ingredients and add to the pan. Heat and season with the white pepper and the 3/4 teaspoon salt.

Serve this soup hot or chilled, garnished with sour cream and minced parsley. Serves 6 to 8.

Note: You may choose to reserve the beet cooking liquid to use instead of the vegetable stock, if you want a fuller beet flavor.

Sweet Potato with Cream Soup

▼▼▼▼▼▼▼▼▼▼▼▼▼▼▼

This soup came one wonderful fall from an abundance of garnet yams (see Note). We ate them at home for weeks; then one day this soup emerged, wonderfully easy to prepare and simply delicious.

It may be served as a rich beginning to a light meal, or sometimes as a dessert.

6 to 9 garnet yams (2 1/2 pounds)
3 cups Simple Vegetable Stock (see page 10)
1 tablespoon unsalted butter
1 cup whipping cream
1/2 cup whipping cream or Simple Vegetable Stock (see page 10)
1/2 teaspoon ginger juice (see page 7)
1/8 teaspoon ground cardamom
Pinch ground cloves
3/4 teaspoon salt, or to taste

Pierce the yams with a knife, place them in a dry pan, and bake in a 400°F oven until they are so soft that sugary syrup is visible, 60 to 75 minutes. Let cool until you can handle the yams comfortably, then peel and set aside. If you find a yellow yam amidst the bright orange ones, save it to eat later, since it would dull the beautiful color of the finished soup.

Pour the 3 cups stock into a blender container, add the peeled yams, and blend until smooth. Transfer to a medium saucepan and stir in all the other ingredients. Heat the soup only until the butter is melted and the soup is hot. Do not boil. Taste for salt and other seasonings, then serve.

This soup is best eaten immediately, but it will keep 1 day, covered in the refrigerator.

Serves 4 to 6.

Note: What we call yams in the United States are really sweet potatoes. Yams are a starchy root native to tropical and subtropical climates.

Mexican Black Bean Soup
▼▼▼▼▼▼▼▼▼▼▼▼▼

Black bean soups evoke strong loyalties. Everyone has a favorite. This is our current one, but please feel free to vary the vegetables and spices to suit your mood.

2 cups black turtle or black mitla beans, sorted and washed
Water, to cover beans
7 cups Simple Vegetable Stock (see page 10) or water
1 onion, finely diced
3 cloves garlic, pressed or minced
1 tablespoon corn or extravirgin olive oil
1 small hot green chile (jalapeño)
or 1 teaspoon ground New Mexico red chile
2 ripe tomatoes, diced medium
1/2 teaspoon ground cumin
1/2 teaspoon black pepper
1/8 teaspoon paprika
1/8 teaspoon cayenne pepper
1/4 teaspoon dried basil
1/2 to 3/4 teaspoon salt, to taste
2 tablespoons minced cilantro
1/4 cup sour cream, optional garnish
1 tablespoon minced red bell pepper, optional garnish
1/4 cup Red Chile Sauce, optional garnish (see page 58)

Soak the beans overnight in the water. Drain and place them in a large saucepan or stockpot with the vegetable stock. Bring the stock and beans to a boil, reduce the heat, and simmer until the beans are tender. Or place the washed beans and the stock in a pressure cooker and cook until tender, approximately 45 minutes. It is important to cook the beans thoroughly before adding any salt or acid ingredients, since these will prevent the beans from softening.

Meanwhile, in a medium saucepan over medium-high heat, saute the onion and garlic in the oil. Stirring occasionally, continue cooking until the onion is sweet and medium brown. Add the chile, diced tomatoes, cumin, black pepper, paprika, cayenne, basil, and 1/2 teaspoon salt. Simmer until the fragrance fills your

Gazpacho

▼▼▼▼▼▼▼▼▼▼▼▼▼

Serve this cooling summer classic with fresh hot tortillas, quesadillas, or crisp corn chips and guacamole.

1 white or yellow onion, diced medium
3 cloves garlic, pressed or minced
1/2 teaspoon salt
1 tablespoon extravirgin olive oil
3 cups Simple Vegetable Stock (see page 10)
9 ripe tomatoes, cored
1 cucumber, trimmed and peeled
2 cups Simple Vegetable Stock (see page 10)
5 ripe tomatoes, finely diced
1 small hot green chile (jalapeño), seeded and minced
1 cucumber, trimmed, peeled, and finely diced
2 mild green chiles (anaheim),
or 1 green bell pepper, seeded and finely diced
1 red bell pepper, finely diced
2 tablespoons minced parsley
2 tablespoons minced cilantro
1/4 cup lemon juice
2 tablespoons lime juice
Salt and black pepper, to taste

Sauté the onion and garlic with the salt in the olive oil until the onion is very sweet and golden brown. Transfer this mixture to blender container, add the 3 cups vegetable stock, and blend until fairly smooth. Pour into a large bowl.

Place the 9 cored tomatoes, the trimmed and peeled cucumber, and the 2 cups stocks in the blender container and blend until almost smooth. (This may need to be done in two batches.) Add this mixture to the stock and onion liquid.

Add the ... d and minced vegetables, herbs, and juices to the sou ... with the salt and black pepper.

Chill and serve. The gazpacho should be cold, tangy, and spicy. It will keep, covered in the refrigerator, for up to 2 days.

Serves 6 to 8.

Chilled Avocado Soup

▼▼▼▼▼▼▼▼▼▼▼▼▼▼

This is a creamy delight. Serve it in cups as the start of any Southwestern or Mexican meal, or in bowls alongside hot quesadillas for lunch.

1 tablespoon lemon juice
1 tablespoon lime juice
2 green onions, trimmed
3 3/4 cups chilled Simple Vegetable Stock (see page 10) or water
1 tablespoon fresh mint leaves
1/2 teaspoon ground cumin
1/8 teaspoon cayenne pepper
1/8 teaspoon white pepper
3/4 teaspoon salt, or to taste
3 large ripe Haas avocados, peeled and seeded
2 tablespoons minced red bell pepper, for garnish
2 tablespoons calendula petals, optional garnish

Place the lemon juice, lime juice, green onions, vegetable stock, mint, spices, and salt in a blender container and blend until smooth. Add the avocados and blend again until just creamy. Chill.

Serve the soup garnished with minced red bell pepper and the calendula petals, if desired.

Avocados are a wonderful food, but they deteriorate rapidly when exposed to the air. Serve this soup within 4 hours of blending.

Serves 4 to 6.

Chilled Cucumber Soup

▼▼▼▼▼▼▼▼▼▼▼▼▼▼

"*Cool as a cucumber*" is an apt description for this light and creamy soup. It is also very easy to prepare.

4 medium cucumbers, trimmed, peeled,
and cut into 1-inch chunks
1/2 cup half-and-half or whole milk
1 tablespoon fresh mint
1 teaspoon fresh dill or fennel, optional
1/2 teaspoon black pepper
3/4 to 1 teaspoon salt, to taste
1/2 cup sour cream or crème fraiche
1 cup plain yogurt
1 teaspoon minced red bell pepper, for garnish
borage blossoms, optional garnish

Place the cucumbers, half-and-half, mint, dill, black pepper, and 3/4 teaspoon salt in a blender container and blend on high until smooth.

In a medium or large bowl, whisk together the sour cream and yogurt. Add approximately 1 cup of the blended cucumber and whisk to combine. Add the rest of the blended cucumber and whisk until smooth. Taste for seasoning.

Chill the soup thoroughly. Serve garnished with the minced red bell pepper or borage blossoms, if desired.

This soup will keep for 1 day covered in the refrigerator.

Serves 4 to 6.

Chilled Honeydew Soup

▼▼▼▼▼▼▼▼▼▼▼▼▼▼▼

When it's too hot to cook, this light and simple soup is easy to prepare and wonderful to eat.

1 ripe honeydew melon, seeded, skinned, and cut into 2-inch chunks
1/4 teaspoon ground cardamom
1 teaspoon lime juice
1/2 teaspoon grated lime zest, for garnish
12 borage blossoms, for garnish

Place the melon, cardamom, and lime juice in a blender container and blend until smooth.

Chill and serve garnished with the lime zest and borage flowers.

This soup is best served the day it is made.

Serves 4 to 6.

Vegetable Accompaniments & Salads

Side dishes, or accompaniments to main dishes, can be as simple as steamed or sautéed vegetables tossed with butter or fresh herbs, or as complex as timbales or soufflés. Here I have chosen the middle road—foods that are not plain, but that are fast and easy to prepare. I hope that they will stimulate your palate and mind so that you will see more possibilities when wandering in your own garden or in the produce market.

Salads are composed in myriad forms, from simple ones to start or accompany a meal, to salads hearty enough for a main dish during the warmer months. Salads are almost always easy to make; they require only fresh, beautiful, and tasty ingredients, put together with a keen eye.

Sugar Snap Peas with Mint Raita

▼▼▼▼▼▼▼▼▼▼▼▼▼▼

Sugar snap peas are one of modern horticulture's success stories. They combine the virtues of English peas and snow peas with edible sweet pods and full-sized peas. They are delicious cooked or raw. Sugar snap peas are not readily available in most grocery stores, but may be found in the spring in gourmet or natural foods store produce departments.

Snap peas are also very easy to grow in most climates. I once planted a spring garden consisting almost entirely of different kinds of peas. I knew that I would be moving from that spot in June and wanted a beautiful and bountiful harvest. My neighbors and I enjoyed many, many delicious peas that year.

This recipe also appears in <u>Santa Fe Lite & Spicy Recipe</u> from Tierra Publications, Joan Stromquist, editor.

2 cups plain yogurt
2 tablespoons minced mint leaves
1/4 teaspoon salt
3/4 cup water
1 pound sugar snap peas, strings removed
1 teaspoon unsalted butter
1/8 teaspoon salt, or to taste

To prepare the raita, in a small bowl whisk together the yogurt, mint, and the 1/4 teaspoon salt. Cover and let it chill in the refrigerator for about 1 hour.

Bring the water to a boil in a medium saucepan. Add the peas; cover and steam only until they turn bright green, 2 to 4 minutes.

Drain the peas and toss with the butter and the 1/8 teaspoon salt. Serve with the chilled raita.

Serves 4 to 6.

Sesame Carrots
and Jerusalem Artichokes

▼▼▼▼▼▼▼▼▼▼▼▼▼▼▼▼

We have a thick stand of Jerusalem artichokes (they don't ever grow any way but thickly!) and, searching for beautiful and tasty ways to serve them, this idea came to me one afternoon.

1 teaspoon light sesame oil
1/2 teaspoon ground turmeric
1 cup sliced or roll-cut carrots
2 1/2 cups Jerusalem artichokes,
peeled and cut into 1/2-inch chunks
1/2 cup water
1/2 to 3/4 teaspoon salt
2 tablespoons toasted white sesame seeds

Heat a medium saucepan over medium heat. Add the sesame oil and turmeric and cook, stirring constantly, until the turmeric is just fragrant but not browned, approximately 30 seconds.

Add the carrots, Jerusalem artichokes, the water, and salt. Simmer, covered, until tender, approximately 10 minutes. Add the toasted sesame seeds and stir to coat the vegetables. Taste for salt and serve.

Serves 4 to 6.

Red Cabbage Balsamico

Thanks to Larry Merica for this idea. It is a tasty, tangy way to serve cabbage and goes very well beside grilled salmon or chicken.

2 cloves garlic, pressed
2 tablespoons extravirgin olive oil
1 pound red cabbage, thinly sliced
1/2 teaspoon salt, or to taste
1/4 teaspoon black pepper
1 to 2 tablespoons balsamic vinegar

Over high heat sauté the garlic in the oil for 15 seconds. Add the cabbage, salt, pepper, and vinegar and continue to cook until the cabbage is tender, 5 to 10 minutes, stirring often.

Serve immediately.

Serves 4 to 6

Ginger Glazed Beets

▼▼▼▼▼▼▼▼▼▼▼▼▼

Beets are one of nature's jewels. Their color and flavor are so rich, they can, in small quantities, be used to enhance other plainer vegetables. Golden beets are a nice change, or can be mixed with red beets for a red and orange dish.

These beets go well with East Indian or other spicy foods. They can also be served with steamed greens and grain for a simple meal.

1 pound red beets, peeled and cut into chunks
3/4 cup water
1 teaspoon peeled and grated or minced fresh ginger
1/4 teaspoon salt
1 to 2 tablespoons pure maple syrup

Place the beets, the water, and ginger in a small saucepan and bring to a boil. Cover and cook over medium heat until the beets are tender.

Add the salt and maple syrup and continue to cook, uncovered, until the liquid is almost gone and the beets are shiny with the glaze. Serve immediately.

Serves 4 to 6.

<u>Variation:</u> Substitute golden beets or carrots for half the red beets.

Green Salad with Two Dressings
▼▼▼▼▼▼▼▼▼▼▼▼▼▼

My favorite salads are fresh greens from the garden in spring. One of the privileges of gardening is to be able to pick the best foods of the season and let them guide your taste and composition.

This is a recipe with no ingredients and no quantities. Simply taste various greens and vegetables and choose your favorite combinations. A few guidelines based on my personal preferences: Balance sweet and bitter greens. One of my favorite combinations is green and red leaf lettuce with mizuna (a beautiful mild Japanese mustard) and frisée (curly endive). Limit the ingredients in a green salad to no more than seven. Like too many cooks, too many greens may spoil the palate.

When you have really good greens, keep the dressing simple. An extravirgin olive oil or light sesame oil paired with freshly squeezed lemon juice and freshly ground black pepper may be all that is required. I have, however, included two slightly more complex dressings for you to try.

Parsley Parmesan Dressing

1 1/4 cups extravirgin olive oil
1/4 cup apple cider vinegar
2 teaspoons pressed garlic
1/2 cup water
3/4 teaspoon dried oregano
3/4 teaspoon dried thyme
3/4 teaspoon black pepper
3/4 teaspoon salt
1 1/4 cups packed parsley leaves
1 tablespoon fresh basil,
or 3/4 teaspoon dried basil
1/2 cup grated Parmesan cheese

Place all the ingredients in a blender container and blend on high only until the parsley is well chopped, with small specks of green still visible.

This dressing will keep its beautiful green color for only 1 day, so plan to use it immediately. If necessary to store, keep covered in the refrigerator.

Makes approximately 2 1/2 cups.

Mustard Vinaigrette Dressing

This dressing recipe works best with all the ingredients at room temperature, but it is not as temperamental as most vinaigrettes.

1 1/2 cups extravirgin olive oil
1/2 cup red wine vinegar or apple cider vinegar
1/4 cup prepared stone-ground mustard
2/3 cup water
2 cloves garlic, pressed
3/4 teaspoon black pepper
1/2 teaspoon salt, or to taste

Place all the ingredients in a blender container and blend on medium-high until the dressing is very smooth and emulsified.

To store, keep covered in the refrigerator for up to 1 week.

Makes approximately 2 1/2 cups.

Japanese Noodle Salad

▼▼▼▼▼▼▼▼▼▼▼▼▼▼

This beautiful summer salad takes some careful vegetable preparation, but it is well worth the effort.

1 cup dried shiitake mushrooms
2 cups water
3 carrots, peeled and cut into 1/8- by 1 1/2-inch matchsticks
2 cups sugar snap peas (strings removed) or snow peas (ends trimmed)
that have been sliced diagonally into 3/4-inch pieces
1 red bell pepper, cut into 1/8- by 2-inch strips
4 green onions, cut into 1/4- by 2-inch strips
2 tablespoons mirin (sweet rice wine)
1 tablespoon soy sauce
2 quarts water, for cooking noodles
Pinch salt
8 ounces somen noodles (see Note)
1 teaspoon light sesame oil
1 tablespoon black sesame seeds, for garnish
4 yellow nasturtium blossoms, for garnish

Soak the shiitake mushrooms overnight in the 2 cups water, or bring to a boil, simmer 10 minutes, cover, and let soak for 1 hour.

Steam each vegetable separately until crisp but tender. Carrots will take the longest time, then the peas, bell pepper, and green onions, respectively. Shock the vegetables in ice water, drain, and chill.

Remove the stems from the soaked mushrooms and discard or save them for another use. Slice the mushrooms very thin (1/16 to 1/8 inch thick). In a heavy skillet braise the mushrooms in the mirin and soy sauce until the liquid is gone and the mushrooms sizzle. Set aside to cool.

Bring the 2 quarts water to a boil. Add a pinch of salt, then drop the noodles into the water gently so that they fall from your hand like a waterfall. Cook only until a small white dot remains in the center of a noodle when cut, 1 to 2 minutes. Immediately drain and shock the noodles in ice water. Drain again and toss gently with the sesame oil. Cover and chill.

To assemble the salad, layer the noodles, steamed vegetables, and braised mushrooms in a medium bowl, topping with a layer of vegetables. Or you may choose to arrange each serving individually.

Immediately before serving, top with the dressing (recipe follows) and garnish with the black sesame seeds and nasturtium blossoms.

This salad must be served the same day it is made, since the noodles will become too soft and the vegetables will lose their color and flavor if stored.

Serves 4.

Note: Somen noodles are thin, light noodles made of sifted wheat flour and salt. They may be found in many natural foods groceries or Asian specialty shops.

Dressing for Japanese Noodle Salad

1/2 cup soy sauce
1/4 cup rice wine vinegar
1 tablespoon ginger juice (see page 7)
1 tablespoon mirin
1/8 teaspoon cayenne pepper, optional

Mix together all the ingredients. Reserve until needed. This dressing will keep several days refrigerated.

Makes 3/4 cup.

Fresh Crab Salad

▼▼▼▼▼▼▼▼▼▼▼▼▼▼▼

Make this salad with crab from a trustworthy fishmonger. Either purchase whole live crabs, boil them, and remove the meat, or buy fresh cooked crabmeat; lump or backfin is the best.

1 small head red leaf lettuce, washed
1 small head green leaf lettuce, washed
1 small head curly endive (frisée), washed, optional
3/4 cup finely diced celery
1/3 cup thinly sliced green onion
1/4 cup finely diced red bell pepper
1/4 cup minced parsley
1/4 teaspoon black pepper
1/8 teaspoon crushed red chile (chile piquin)
1/4 cup lemon juice
1/4 cup lime juice
1/4 cup extravirgin olive oil
1/2 teaspoon salt
1 1/2 pounds fresh cooked crabmeat, chilled
1 small head radicchio, washed
5 ripe tomatoes, cored and quartered
Borage blossoms, optional garnish

Dry the leafy vegetables. Tear the lettuces and curly endive into bite-sized pieces. Keep cold.

Mix together the celery, green onion, red bell pepper, parsley, black pepper, red chile, lemon and lime juices, olive oil, and salt. Toss this dressing with the crabmeat.

To serve the salad, arrange the greens on chilled plates. Top each salad with a medium-sized radicchio leaf. Place a mound of the mixed crab salad in each radicchio leaf. Place 4 or 5 tomato wedges on each salad, either arranging them with their points together, like a flower, or symmetrically around the edge of the plate. Garnish the salads with the borage blossoms, and serve.

Serves 4.

Artichoke Rice Salad

▼▼▼▼▼▼▼▼▼▼▼▼▼

Martha Henderson, who co-owned The Harvest Cafe in Oxford, Mississippi, came up with this recipe. It is a cooling salad with varied flavors that can be served as a light summer meal.

1 1/2 cups basmati rice

3 cups water

1/2 teaspoon salt

1/4 teaspoon ground turmeric

2 tablespoons unsalted butter

1 tablespoon lemon juice

1/2 teaspoon pressed garlic

1/2 cup finely diced red onion

1/2 cup pitted black olives

1/2 cup minced parsley

1 teaspoon salt

1/2 teaspoon black pepper

1 cup diced ripe tomatoes

6 cups washed mixed greens (lettuce and chicory)

8 ounces marinated artichoke hearts

2 calendula blossoms, petals only, optional garnish

Wash the rice thoroughly in cool water until the water becomes clear. Drain and set aside. In a medium saucepan bring the water to a boil with the 1/2 teaspoon salt and turmeric. Add the rice and bring once again to a boil. Add the butter, reduce the heat to low, cover, and cook until the water is gone and the rice is fluffy, approximately 20 minutes. Keep the pan covered at least 15 minutes or until completely cool. This resting period is necessary for the grains to completely absorb the moisture and to retain their shape when stirred later. The rice may be cooked up to 1 day before assembling the salad.

Mix together the lemon juice, garlic, onion, olives, parsley, the 1 teaspoon salt, pepper, and tomatoes. Stir this mixture gently into the cool rice. Chill from 30 minutes to 3 hours to allow the flavors to mingle. Serve the rice salad on a bed of greens. Arrange the marinated artichoke hearts around the mound of rice. Garnish with calendula petals, if desired.

Serves 4 to 6.

Dijon Chicken Salad

▼▼▼▼▼▼▼▼▼▼▼▼▼▼▼

This hearty salad makes a satisfying luncheon meal or a beautiful appetizer. Take care when arranging the salads on the serving plates and the results will be spectacular.

2 pounds skinless, boneless chicken breasts
1 tablespoon extravirgin olive oil
1 tablespoon lemon juice
1/2 teaspoon black pepper
4 cups mixed greens, washed and chilled
4 radicchio leaves
1 cup sugar snap or snow peas, blanched and chilled (see Note)
1/2 cup finely diced celery
1 medium cucumber, peeled and thinly sliced
4 ripe tomatoes, cored and quartered
2 tablespoons finely slivered green onion, for garnish
2 tablespoons finely diced red bell pepper, for garnish
4 nasturtium blossoms or 12 tangerine gem marigold blossoms,
optional garnish

Wash the chicken in cold water and drain thoroughly. Mix the olive oil, lemon juice, and black pepper; place the chicken in this marinade for 1 to 2 hours. Grill or broil the chicken until it is tender but no longer pink. Cut the cooked chicken into 1/4-inch-thick slices and chill.

To assemble the salads, arrange the mixed greens over each radicchio leaf on 4 chilled plates. Top with the chicken, peas, and celery arranged in a wheel pattern or with artful abandon. Add the cucumbers and tomatoes.

Ladle the dressing (recipe follows) over each salad in a thick line or zigzag pattern. Top with the green onion, red bell pepper, and flower garnish, if desired. Serve immediately.

Serves 4.

Note: Blanching is essentially parboiling. It is used here to slightly cook and set the color of the peas. Drop the washed peas into a pot of boiling water and cook just until the color is bright green. Immediately drain the peas and shock them by plunging them into an ice water bath, which will set their vibrant color.

Creamy Dijon Dressing

1/2 cup sour cream
3 tablespoons Dijon mustard
3 tablespoons lemon juice
1/4 cup extravirgin olive oil
1/4 teaspoon black pepper
1/4 teaspoon white pepper
1/2 teaspoon salt
1 tablespoon minced fresh tarragon

Whisk together the sour cream, mustard, and lemon juice. Add the olive oil, black and white pepper, salt, and tarragon and continue whisking until smooth.
Makes 1 cup.

Salsas, Sauces, and Chutneys

These mixtures can serve as the basis of a meal or as the seasoning that brings out the perfect flavor of a well-cooked food. They are not meant to cover up but to enhance. Keep this in mind when working on new combinations of ingredients.

Before cooking, I often visualize with my tasting imagination. Everyone has this faculty; practice develops it and the confidence to use it. To check on my perception, I may try a small bit of sauce on a bite of pea or cooked chicken. I am often amazed and delighted at the combinations that really work. One note of caution: There has been some fashion in recent years of unorthodox food combinations just for the sake of variety. When flavors and foods don't belong together they may taste interesting for a moment, but the lasting impression will not leave your mouth with a delicious taste and may leave your stomach in even worse shape. When cooking with compatible foods and spices, your mouth will tingle with a wonderful feeling. We have all had that exquisite experience. Reach for it!

East Indian Coconut Sauce
▼▼▼▼▼▼▼▼▼▼▼▼▼

White fish such as halibut, grouper, mahi mahi, or sea bass are delicious simmered in this sauce. It may also be served over fish that has been grilled with light sesame oil and lemon juice.

3 cloves garlic, pressed
1 tablespoon unsalted butter
1 small white or yellow onion, finely diced
1/4 teaspoon salt
1/4 teaspoon ground turmeric
1 teaspoon ground New Mexico red chile or
1/8 teaspoon cayenne pepper
1/4 cup unsweetened shredded coconut
1/2 teaspoon salt
1/2 cup water or Simple Vegetable Stock (see page 10)
1/2 cup whipping cream
Pinch ground cardamom
1/4 teaspoon lemon juice or 1/8 teaspoon mango powder (see Note)

In a small saucepan over medium-heat, sauté the garlic in the butter until golden. Add the onion and the 1/4 teaspoon salt. Continue cooking until the onion is very sweet and lightly browned. Add the turmeric, red chile, coconut, and the 1/2 teaspoon salt. Cook only until the coconut is fragrant but not browned.

Pour the coconut mixture into a blender container, add the water, and blend on high until creamy. Stir in the cream, cardamom, and lemon juice. Taste for salt and spice.

Use immediately or store refrigerated for 1 to 2 days.

Makes approximately 1 1/2 cups.

Note: Mango powder may be purchased at East Indian specialty stores, occasionally at a full-service natural foods store. It is made from unripe mango.

Lime Salsa Fresca

▼▼▼▼▼▼▼▼▼▼▼▼▼▼

Salsas can vary from the simple combination of a few ingredients to complex creations. The sublime flavor of this one from Larry Merica depends on summer ripe tomatoes and chiles and uniformly diced vegetables.

This salsa is delightful as a dip or topping for vegetarian enchiladas or a bowl of beans. It is also a very tasty topping for barbecued chicken.

2 small hot green chiles (jalapeño), seeded and minced
3 medium red ripe tomatoes, finely diced
3 medium yellow or 12 yellow pear tomatoes, finely diced
2 cloves garlic, pressed
1/3 cup minced red onion
1/3 cup lime juice
3/4 teaspoon salt
1/2 teaspoon black pepper
1 1/2 tablespoons minced cilantro

Combine all of the ingredients and allow to stand at least 2 hours before serving. The salsa is best served the same day it is made.

Makes 2 cups.

Tomatillo Salsa

▼▼▼▼▼▼▼▼▼▼▼▼▼▼▼

This piquant salsa makes a good dip. It is equally good on grilled chicken or fresh white fish, especially halibut or sea bass.

3 cloves garlic, minced
1 tablespoon unsalted butter
1/2 pound tomatillos, husked, washed, and finely diced
1 small hot green chile (jalapeño), seeded and minced
1/2 red bell pepper, seeded and minced
3 tablespoons lime juice
1/4 teaspoon black pepper
3 tablespoons minced cilantro
1/2 teaspoon salt

Sauté the garlic in the butter until fragrant and golden. Add the tomatillos, chile, bell pepper, lime juice, and black pepper. Cook over high heat only until the tomatillos turn brilliant green. Remove from the heat and add the cilantro and salt.

Serve at room temperature. The salsa is best used immediately.

Makes 1 cup.

Tomato Basil Sauce

▼▼▼▼▼▼▼▼▼▼▼▼▼▼▼

This recipe was inspired by a Japanese chef who generously allowed me into his restaurant kitchen to study for a week. He and his staff were most gracious and I learned an immense amount in that short time.

The success of the sauce depends on fresh basil and summer ripe tomatoes for its luscious flavor. Serve it hot over freshly cooked pasta topped with grated Parmesan or Romano cheese. It is also very good on grilled chicken or yellowfin tuna.

4 cloves garlic, pressed or minced
1 tablespoon extravirgin olive oil
1 small white or yellow onion, finely diced
1/2 teaspoon salt, or to taste
9 ripe plum tomatoes or 6 ripe medium tomatoes,
cored and diced, peeled if desired
1/4 cup dry white wine
1/4 teaspoon black pepper, or to taste
1/4 teaspoon dried basil
1/2 teaspoon minced fresh oregano,
or 1/4 teaspoon dried oregano
1/4 cup minced fresh basil

In a nonreactive medium saucepan, sauté the garlic in the olive oil until golden. Add the onion and salt and cook over medium-high heat, stirring frequently, until the onion is very sweet and dark golden brown.

Add the tomatoes, wine, black pepper, and dried basil. Simmer until the liquid is reduced by one fourth and the flavors meld, 20 to 40 minutes.

Add the oregano and fresh basil. Immediately remove from the heat, and add salt and black pepper to taste.

With its emphasis on fresh herbs, this sauce is best served the same day it is made. If desired, it can be prepared up to 1 day ahead, but add the fresh oregano and fresh basil just before serving.

Makes approximately 3 cups.

Tomato Chutney
▼▼▼▼▼▼▼▼▼▼▼▼▼

This simple chutney is an appropriately spicy accompaniment to basmati rice and lentils. It also makes a fine sauce for grilled chicken.

1/2 pound ripe tomatoes
1/2 teaspoon peeled and minced fresh ginger
1 clove garlic, pressed or minced
1/4 teaspoon ground turmeric
Pinch cayenne pepper
1/4 teaspoon black mustard seed
1 1/2 tablespoons light sesame oil
2 cloves garlic, pressed or minced
1/2 teaspoon cumin seed
1/8 teaspoon fenugreek seed
1 small dried red chile,
or 1/4 teaspoon crushed red chile (chile piquin)
1/3 teaspoon salt, or to taste

In a small nonreactive bowl, mix together the diced tomatoes, ginger, the clove of pressed garlic, turmeric, and cayenne pepper. Let stand for at least 15 minutes.

Over high heat, toast the black mustard seeds in the sesame oil only until the seeds pop and turn gray (see Note). Immediately reduce the heat to medium-high and add the 2 cloves pressed garlic, cumin, and fenugreek. Continue cooking until the garlic is fragrant and golden brown.

Reduce the heat to medium and add the chile; stir and cook 15 seconds. Add the tomato mixture and the salt. Increase the heat to medium-high and continue to cook until the sauce has thickened slightly but the diced tomatoes still hold their shape, approximately 10 minutes. Taste for salt.

Serve immediately or keep covered in the refrigerator for up to 2 days.

Makes approximately 2/3 cup.

Note: Black mustard seeds add a delicious flavor and depth when sautéed or roasted until they pop and turn light gray. However, if not cooked long enough, they will impart an unpleasant bitterness to any dish. If permitted to turn black, please begin again, since the burned flavor they impart is very unappealing.

Sun-Dried Tomato Pesto

▼▼▼▼▼▼▼▼▼▼▼▼▼▼

Sun-dried tomatoes have a tangy, sweet flavor that especially enhances yellow fin tuna, any firm white fish, or chicken. This simple pesto is also a wonderful addition to homemade pizza or as a pasta sauce.

1/4 cup boiling water
1 cup sun-dried tomatoes (not packed in olive oil)
5 cloves garlic
1/3 cup extravirgin olive oil
1/4 teaspoon black pepper
1/4 teaspoon crushed red chile (chile piquin)
1 teaspoon balsamic vinegar
1 tablespoon chopped fresh basil
3/4 teaspoon salt

Pour the boiling water over the sun-dried tomatoes. Cover and let stand 15 minutes.

Place all the ingredients in the bowl of a food processor and blend only until chunky. Or mash the garlic with a mortar and pestle; add the soaked tomatoes and grind them into small chunks; mince the basil and add with the remaining ingredients.

Use immediately or refrigerate for up to 1 week.

Makes 1 cup.

Toasted Almond Pesto

▼▼▼▼▼▼▼▼▼▼▼▼▼

A wonderful cook named Carol is responsible for this dish. It is delicious on hot pita bread, grilled chicken, or any white fish. Try it tossed with lightly steamed green beans for a tasty side dish.

1/2 cup shelled almonds
1 tablespoon pressed garlic
1/3 cup extravirgin olive oil
1 tablespoon dry white wine
1/3 teaspoon salt
1/4 teaspoon cayenne pepper
1/4 teaspoon paprika

Roast the almonds in a dry pan in a 350°F oven until the skins begin to crack and the meat is golden brown, 5 to 10 minutes. Let cool completely.

Mix together the garlic, olive oil, and white wine. Add the salt, cayenne, and paprika.

Chop the toasted almonds into fine pieces or blend briefly (pulsing) in a dry blender or food processor. Add to the other ingredients and mix well.

This pesto should be used directly after it is made, since the almonds lose their crunchiness after 1 day. Refrigerate the pesto if not using within 1 hour.

Makes 1/2 cup.

Walnut Tapenade

▼▼▼▼▼▼▼▼▼▼▼▼▼

Roasting nuts transforms them. It brings out their flavor, cuts their sharpness, and, with walnuts especially, emphasizes their creaminess. Toss this tapenade sparingly with pasta and steamed vegetables for a simple and satisfying meal.

2 1/4 cups walnut halves
1 cup extravirgin olive oil
1/3 cup peeled garlic cloves
1 tablespoon prepared stone-ground mustard
3/4 teaspoon black pepper
1/2 teaspoon salt
2 tablespoons capers
2 teaspoons minced fresh rosemary or 3/4 teaspoon dried rosemary

Roast the walnuts in a dry pan in a 350°F oven only until fragrant and very lightly browned, 5 to 8 minutes. Let cool.

Blend the olive oil, garlic, mustard, pepper, and salt in a blender or food processor until smooth, or press the garlic and mix the ingredients by hand.

Add 2 cups of the cooled toasted walnuts, the capers, and the rosemary and process very briefly if using an electric appliance, or chop the nuts and capers fine and stir with the rosemary into the olive-garlic mixture. The tapenade should be slightly chunky, not pasty.

Serve tossed with freshly cooked pasta and vegetables or spread on hot pita bread. Garnish with the reserved 1/4 cup toasted nuts.

The tapenade will keep up to 2 days refrigerated.

Makes 2 cups.

Buttered Pecans

▼▼▼▼▼▼▼▼▼▼▼▼▼

Yes, I love nuts. When I was a pure vegetarian I finally learned not to feel guilty for eating them. Nuts contain protein and have a wonderful flavor. These buttered pecans make a delicious sauce for pasta. They are also very good on broiled chicken or on any grilled white fish. If serving the nuts this way, cook the fish or chicken with lemon to bring out a bright flavor.

1 1/2 cups pecan halves
1/4 cup unsalted butter
1 medium white or yellow onion, finely diced
2 cloves garlic, pressed
1/8 teaspoon cayenne pepper
1/2 teaspoon salt
3/4 cup unsalted butter
1/4 cup grated Asiago or Parmesan cheese, optional garnish

In a dry baking pan, roast the pecans in a 325°F oven until fragrant but not browned, 5 to 8 minutes. Let cool, then chop.

Melt the 1/4 cup butter in a heavy-bottomed skillet. Add the onion, garlic, cayenne, and salt and sauté over medium-high heat until the onion is very sweet and golden brown.

Add the 3/4 cup butter and melt over low heat. Do not brown.

Just before serving, add the roasted pecans to the butter mixture. If serving as a pasta sauce, garnish with the grated cheese.

These nuts may be prepared up to 1 day ahead, provided that the butter mixture is kept refrigerated and the nuts are kept cool and dry.

Makes 2 1/2 cups; serves 6 as a pasta sauce.

Lemon Caper Sauce

▼▼▼▼▼▼▼▼▼▼▼▼▼▼▼

Capers are the pickled immature flower buds of a Mediterranean shrub. Pickled nasturtium buds can be substituted for capers. Serve this sauce at room temperature on grilled fish or chicken. It may also be used as a tangy dressing for a summer salad, and goes especially well with ripe tomatoes.

1/4 cup lemon juice
1 1/2 teaspoons Dijon mustard
3 cloves garlic, pressed
1/2 cup extravirgin olive oil, at room temperature
3 tablespoons minced red bell pepper
1/2 cup drained capers (preferably small ones)
1/8 teaspoon dried thyme
1/8 teaspoon black pepper
1/8 teaspoon salt

In a small bowl mix together the lemon juice, mustard, and garlic. Slowly whisk in the olive oil, pouring in a thin stream, until the sauce begins to emulsify, 1 to 2 minutes. Stir in the red bell pepper, capers, thyme, black pepper, and salt. Taste for seasoning.

This sauce is best used within 1 day of being prepared. If you wish to keep it longer, simply omit the red bell pepper until just before using. Keep covered in the refrigerator.

Makes 1 1/2 cups.

Mango Curry Sauce

▼▼▼▼▼▼▼▼▼▼▼▼▼▼▼

This elegantly simple sauce was first served to me over steamed basmati rice by an Indian friend. It makes a deliciously cooling light meal on a summer's day.

1 tablespoon unsalted butter
1 teaspoon cumin seed
1 to 2 small hot green chiles (jalapeño), seeded and minced
2 teaspoons peeled and minced fresh ginger
3 large or 4 medium ripe mangoes, peeled and diced
1/2 teaspoon salt, or to taste
2 tablespoons minced cilantro
1/4 teaspoon lemon juice, optional

In a nonreactive skillet or saucepan, melt the butter. Add the cumin and sauté over medium-high heat until fragrant, approximately 1 minute.

Add the chiles and ginger and cook only until the chiles are bright green and slightly crisp. Add the mango and continue cooking only until the sauce is heated through. Add salt to taste; stir in the cilantro and the lemon juice, if desired.

As with most fruit sauces, this is best served the same day it is made.

Makes approximately 2 cups.

Persimmon Glaze

▼▼▼▼▼▼▼▼▼▼▼▼▼

*O*ne November, we stayed for a week in a small guesthouse in the hills of Santa Barbara. Each evening my parents would give us a small box of ripe persimmons to take home. We ate these persimmons for breakfast, watching the dog run in the field below. They were so sweet and luscious. My love of this fruit grew each day.

Persimmons are of two types, astringent and nonastringent. Astringent persimmons lose their "bite" and become sweet when they are very soft (translucent and gelatinous). Nonastringent persimmons may be eaten when hard, like an apple, or they may be allowed to ripen. In my opinion, astringent persimmons are the most flavorful, but if you are impatient and eat one before its time, you may never want to try again. Hachiya persimmons are the most commonly sold astringent type. American persimmons, also astringent but much smaller in size than Hachiyas, grow throughout the southeastern United States. They are also delicious when ripe, and may be used in any recipe calling for Oriental persimmons. Approximately five American persimmons will equal the yield from one Hachiya persimmon.

This glaze is wonderful on chicken and would be a fine accompaniment to roast turkey.

4 to 6 very ripe Hachiya persimmons,
or enough to make 1 1/2 cups pulp
1 1/2 teaspoons lemon juice
3/4 teaspoon grated lemon zest
1/4 teaspoon white pepper
Pinch salt
1 to 2 tablespoons sweet white wine (a dessert wine would be perfect)

Peel the persimmons, remove any seeds, and mash the pulp (or blend and strain the pulp). Doing this by hand is slightly slower but yields a nicer texture and flavor.

Add the remaining ingredients and mix well. Serve at room temperature.

This is a quick and easy sauce to make, so I recommend doing it immediately before serving.

Makes 1 1/2 cups.

Pomegranate Glaze

▼▼▼▼▼▼▼▼▼▼▼▼▼▼▼

Serve this glaze over broiled fresh fish. The seeds sparkle like jewels and appear especially beautiful at Christmas.

2 green onions, roughly chopped
1 cup red wine
1/2 teaspoon whole black peppercorns
1 bay leaf
2 pomegranates
1/2 cup water
2 tablespoons unsalted butter
1 teaspoon pure maple syrup
1/4 teaspoon salt
2 teaspoons arrowroot dissolved in 1/4 cup water

In a small nonreactive saucepan, simmer the green onion, wine, peppercorns, and bay leaf until the mixture is reduced by half. Strain and reserve the liquid.

Meanwhile, peel and seed the pomegranates. Reserve 1/2 cup of the seeds for garnish. Blend the remaining seeds with the water, then strain through a fine sieve.

Add this pomegranate juice, butter, maple syrup, and salt to the wine reduction. Simmer for 5 minutes.

Add the arrowroot mixture to the glaze, stirring well, and simmer only until the sauce becomes clear and slightly thickened. Serve the glaze over broiled fish and garnish with the reserved seeds.

For the best results, make this simple sauce right before serving.

Makes approximately 1 1/3 cups.

Raspberry Plum Glaze

▼▼▼▼▼▼▼▼▼▼▼▼▼

In the late summer an abundance of fresh raspberries from Mora County graces the tables of Santa Fe. If it has been a good year, wonderful purple plums ripen at the same time. Together, they make an astonishing sauce for grilled or barbecued chicken. This recipe also appears in <u>Santa Fe Lite and Spicy Recipe</u> from Tierra publications, Joan Stromquist, editor.

2 cups halved and pitted red or purple plums
1 cup red wine
1/8 teaspoon salt
1/4 teaspoon black pepper
1 cup fresh raspberries

Simmer the plums and wine in a small nonreactive saucepan until the plums are very tender, approximately 15 minutes. Put the mixture through a food mill to remove the skins.

Add the salt and pepper and 1/2 cup of the raspberries to the plum sauce. Serve hot over grilled chicken, using the remaining 1/2 cup of berries for garnish.

The plum and wine mixture may be made up to 1 day ahead and kept refrigerated. Add the berries immediately before use or they will lose their firm texture.

Makes 2 cups.

Ginger Apricot Chutney

▼▼▼▼▼▼▼▼▼▼▼▼▼▼

Here in the high desert, apricot trees flourish. In the years when the spring blossoms aren't nipped by the frost, the apricot bounty is so abundant that the fruit can be swept off the streets. After apricot cobbler, apricot ice cream, and many sun-warmed apricots right off the tree for breakfast, I was driven to find other ways to enjoy this wonderful fruit. This chutney is a delicious accompaniment to grilled chicken or roast turkey.

1/3 teaspoon cumin seed
1 1/2 tablespoons peeled and grated fresh ginger
1 tablespoon light sesame oil
2 cups firm ripe apricots cut into 1/4-inch chunks
1 small hot green chile (jalapeño), seeded and minced
1/2 cup orange juice
1/4 teaspoon salt
1/4 cup minced red or sweet white onion
1 teaspoon honey or pure maple syrup, optional

Sauté the cumin and ginger in the sesame oil until fragrant. Add the apricots, chile, orange juice, and salt. Simmer only until tender, about 5 minutes. Remove from the heat and add the minced onion. If you like a sweeter chutney, honey or maple syrup may be added. This chutney will keep several days refrigerated. Serve at room temperature.

Makes 1 1/2 to 2 cups.

Main Dishes

Just as a clean and quiet room with fresh flowers on the table and companions of good cheer and hearty appetites are the aesthetic and spiritual centers of any meal, the main dish is the focus of the meal, in fragrance, flavor, and substance.

Paradoxically, I often put together meals at home with no real "main dish," but then the separate smaller dishes grow together to become the entrée. You may easily do this with many of the recipes in this book, but this chapter is reserved for those special dishes that stand on their own as a focal point.

The main dishes presented here vary in preparation time from the quick-and-easy to those that require beginning the meal the day before. For those of you unfamiliar with vegetarian dishes as main dishes, I hope that some of these recipes will open up a new culinary world for you and inspire new adaptations of familiar foods.

Grilled Polenta with Red Chile Sauce & Black Beans

▼▼▼▼▼▼▼▼▼▼▼▼▼▼

Polenta is warming and satisfying. To get the maximum flavor, I have found that it is best to toast the cornmeal first and then to cook it really thoroughly. This brings out the sweetness and makes it easy to digest.

I serve this version of grilled polenta with red chile sauce and black beans with sour cream. It is also very good, and more traditional, topped with Tomato Basil Sauce (see page 44) and accompanied by steamed or sautéed summer squash.

The polenta needs to cool completely before it is sliced, so plan to make it in the morning to serve it at night, or cook it the day before serving.

1 teaspoon extravirgin olive oil, for oiling pan
2 1/2 cups stone-ground yellow cornmeal
3 cups cold water
3/4 teaspoon salt
2 3/4 cups cold water
1/4 cup grated Parmesan cheese
2 tablespoons unsalted butter, melted
1/2 teaspoon extravirgin olive oil
2 to 4 tablespoons extravirgin olive oil,
or unsalted butter, for grilling

Oil a 4- by 8-in loaf pan with the 1 teaspoon olive oil. Set aside.

Toast the cornmeal over medium heat in a heavy skillet until it is fragrant but not browned. Immediately pour the cornmeal into a bowl and let cool.

In a medium heavy-bottomed saucepan, bring the 3 cups water and the salt to a boil.

Whisk together the cooled cornmeal and the 2 3/4 cups water. Pour this mixture into the boiling water, stirring constantly. When the polenta begins to boil, cover the pot and reduce the heat to low. Cook the polenta until it is very thick and soft, 45 to 55 minutes.

Stir in the Parmesan cheese and melted butter, then spoon the polenta into the oiled pan, pressing the polenta firmly into the pan using either your hand or a spoon that has been dipped in cold water. Sprinkle on the 1/2 teaspoon olive oil and rub it over the surface of the polenta.

Let the polenta cool, then cover it with waxed paper or plastic wrap and store in the refrigerator until you are ready to grill it. It will keep this way for 2 days.

To grill the polenta, invert the pan onto a cutting board and tap firmly. The polenta may come out the first time, but if not, simply run a knife around the edge of the pan and try again.

Slice the polenta into twelve 1/2-inch pieces. Rinse or wipe the knife with cold water between each cut.

In a heavy skillet over medium-high heat, grill the polenta slices in the 2 to 4 tablespoons olive oil until they are golden and crisp on both sides. Serve immediately with Red Chile Sauce (recipe follows) or a sauce of your choice.

Serves 6.

Variation 1: To make a spicier polenta to serve with Tomato Basil Sauce, sauté the polenta with fresh garlic and black pepper.

Variation 2: For a simple and satisfying breakfast, omit the Parmesan cheese when preparing the polenta, then sauté the slices in butter and top with warm maple syrup or honey.

Red Chile Sauce

5 cloves garlic, pressed
2 tablespoons extravirgin olive oil
2 tablespoons yellow cornmeal
1/2 cup ground New Mexico red chile
2 1/2 cups Simple Vegetable Stock (see page 10)
or water (see Note)
1/4 teaspoon black pepper
1/8 teaspoon dried oregano
2 tablespoons unsalted butter
3/4 teaspoon salt

In a medium saucepan over medium heat, sauté the garlic in the olive oil until golden. Add the cornmeal and cook 1 minute, stirring constantly.

Add the red chile and continue cooking only until fragrant. Do not let the chile brown or the sauce will taste bitter.

Remove the pan from the heat and slowly whisk in the stock, then bring the sauce to a boil over medium heat. Reduce the heat and simmer 10 to 15 minutes.

Add the black pepper, oregano, butter, and salt and simmer until the flavors mingle, 5 to 10 minutes more.

This sauce will keep, covered in the refrigerator, for up to 4 days.

Makes 3 cups.

Note: Please use stock if possible. Although the sauce tastes good made with water, the flavor is much richer when the sauce is made with vegetable stock.

Black Beans

2 cups black turtle or black mitla beans,
sorted and washed
5 to 7 cups water
1 clove garlic, pressed
1/8 teaspoon peeled and grated fresh ginger
1/8 teaspoon ground New Mexico red chile
1 teaspoon ground cumin
Pinch nutmeg
1 teaspoon salt

Soak the beans in the water overnight before cooking, or bring the beans and water to a boil, cook for 5 minutes, then let stand for 1 hour before proceeding.

Cook the beans in a large saucepan until they are quite tender but still whole, 1 to 2 hours. Or you may cook the beans with 5 cups water in a pressure cooker until done, approximately 45 minutes. Make sure that the beans are done before seasoning them, because the salt will inhibit further softening.

Add the remaining ingredients to the cooked beans and stir well. Serve hot.

Serves 6.

Vegetarian Texas Chili
with Lime Sour Cream

▼▼▼▼▼▼▼▼▼▼▼▼▼

Texas chili is usually made with meat, so this may be a contradiction in terms. It is, however, very full-bodied and filling. Serve the chili steaming hot and topped with sour cream and ripe avocado slices. Accompany the chili with hot tortillas or fresh cornbread.

1 cup pinto beans, sorted and washed
2 1/2 to 4 cups water, depending on cooking method
1 tablespoon corn oil
1 small yellow onion, finely diced
1 to 2 teaspoons minced garlic
1/4 teaspoon ground New Mexico red chile
1 small hot green chile (jalapeño), seeded and minced
1 mild green chile (anaheim), seeded and finely diced
1 red bell pepper, seeded and finely diced
1 cup diced tomato
1 1/2 teaspoons ground cumin
1 teaspoon ground coriander
3/4 to 1 teaspoon salt, to taste
2 teaspoons minced fresh oregano,
or 3/4 teaspoon dried oregano
2 tablespoons minced cilantro
1/3 cup grated Monterey jack,
or mild Cheddar cheese, for garnish
1/3 cup Lime Sour Cream,
or plain sour cream, for garnish
1 ripe avocado, sliced just before serving, for garnish
1 tablespoon cilantro leaves or chives, for garnish

Soak the beans overnight in water to cover. Drain the beans and place them in a large saucepan with the 4 cups water. Bring the water to a boil, reduce the heat, and simmer until the beans are tender. Or place the washed beans and the 2 1/2 cups water in a small pressure cooker and cook until tender, approximately

30 minutes. It is important to cook the beans thoroughly before adding any salt or acid ingredients, since these will prevent the beans from cooking further.

Meanwhile, warm a heavy skillet over medium-high heat. Add the corn oil, onion, and garlic and sauté until the onion is sweet and golden brown. Add the red chile, hot and mild green chiles, red bell pepper, tomato, cumin, coriander, and salt. Continue to cook until the green chiles are bright green and fragrant.

Add this onion mixture to the cooked beans and simmer for approximately 10 minutes. Stir in the oregano and minced cilantro. Taste for salt.

Spoon the chili into wide bowls. Top it first with the grated cheese, then the Lime Sour Cream and avocado slices. Sprinkle on the cilantro leaves and serve.

The chili is best eaten the day it is made, but it will keep, covered in the refrigerator, for 1 to 2 days.

Serves 4 to 6.

Lime Sour Cream

1/3 cup sour cream
1/8 teaspoon grated lime zest
1 teaspoon lime juice
1/8 teaspoon paprika
Pinch black pepper
Pinch salt

Mix all the ingredients together. If you make this ahead of time, keep refrigerated.

Makes 1/3 cup.

Spinach Enchiladas with Chile Cheese Sauce

▼▼▼▼▼▼▼▼▼▼▼▼▼▼

Martha Flannery created this dish. It is moderately spicy and rich with the Chile Cheese Sauce, but these days I serve it most often with Red Chile Sauce (see page 58) for a lighter feeling and the wonderful color contrast. Serve these rolled enchiladas, two per person, with black or pinto beans and a green salad.

2 bunches fresh spinach, washed
and blanched (see Note)
1 yellow onion, finely diced
2 cloves garlic, pressed or minced
1 tablespoon extravirgin olive oil
1 small hot green chile (jalapeño),
seeded and minced, optional
1 teaspoon cumin seed
1/4 teaspoon salt
1 cup coarsely grated Monterey jack cheese
3 tablespoons finely grated Parmesan cheese
1/2 cup sour cream
1/4 teaspoon black pepper
1/4 teaspoon white pepper
1/4 teaspoon salt
12 corn tortillas
1/4 to 1/3 cup corn oil, for frying tortillas

Roughly chop the blanched spinach and place in a medium bowl. Reserve.

Sauté the onions and garlic in the olive oil over medium-high heat until the onion is light golden. Stir only as often as necessary to keep the onion from sticking. (Too much stirring will result in mushy onions.) Add the green chile, if desired, cumin seed, and 1/4 teaspoon salt. Sauté until the cumin seed is fragrant and the onion is very sweet. Set aside to cool.

Add the cheeses, sour cream, black and white pepper, and 1/4 teaspoon salt to the spinach. Add the cooled onion mixture and stir until well blended.

On a griddle or in a skillet over high heat, cook the tortillas in the corn oil only until soft and slightly puffy, approximately 30 seconds on each side. Spoon 2 rounded tablespoons of filling onto each tortilla. Roll the enchilada firmly and place seam side down in a lightly oiled baking dish. At this point, you may cook the enchiladas or cover and refrigerate them for up to 4 hours before serving. Longer refrigeration will cause the tortillas to dry out and crack.

Preheat the oven to 400°F. Cover the ends of the enchiladas with the sauce of your choice (this will take about 1 1/4 cups sauce), and bake until the sauce is bubbling and the enchiladas are hot, 15 to 20 minutes. To serve, arrange 2 hot enchiladas per person on warmed plates and cover with the remaining sauce.

Serves 6.

Note: To blanch the spinach, bring a large pot of water to a boil. Add the washed spinach and cook over high heat only until the spinach turns bright green. Drain and reserve.

Chile Cheese Sauce

1/3 cup unbleached white flour
1/3 cup Simple Vegetable Stock (see page 10) or water
1 cup whipping cream
1/3 cup half-and-half or milk
3/4 cup coarsely grated Monterey jack cheese
1/4 teaspoon white pepper
2 small hot green chiles (jalapeño), seeded and minced,
or 2 mild green chiles (anaheim), seeded and finely diced
1 tablespoon extravirgin olive oil
Pinch ground nutmeg
2 tablespoons minced cilantro
1/4 teaspoon salt

In a heavy saucepan over medium heat, dry-roast the flour, stirring constantly, until it is fragrant but not browned. Remove from the heat. Immediately mix together the stock, cream, and half-and-half. Slowly add the liquid to the flour, whisking constantly until smooth.

Add the cheese and white pepper and cook over low heat until the cheese melts (it will become stringy for a few minutes but will soon smooth out).

Meanwhile, sauté the chiles of your choice in the olive oil until bright green and slightly crisp. Add these to the sauce.

Just before serving, add the nutmeg, cilantro, and salt.

Makes approximately 2 1/2 cups.

Millet-Stuffed Winter Squash

▼▼▼▼▼▼▼▼▼▼▼▼▼

This sounds like a very banal dish, something one might feed to birds. However, when artfully prepared and accompanied by black beans and sauteed greens, it makes an elegant vegetarian meal. Of course, it can be served as a filling side dish.

This is not difficult to make, but it does require advance planning, since the millet is best when soaked overnight.

3/4 cup millet, covered with cool water
and soaked 6 to 10 hours
2 1/2 cups water
1/4 teaspoon salt
2 small winter squash (honey delight,
gold nugget, or delicata are good)
1 medium yellow onion, finely diced
2 tablespoons unsalted butter or light sesame oil
1/8 teaspoon ground turmeric
3/4 teaspoon cumin seed
1/4 teaspoon klonji (see Note)
1 small hot green chile (jalapeño), seeded and minced
1 stalk celery, finely diced
1/2 teaspoon salt, or to taste
1/4 cup chopped pecans
2 tablespoons minced parsley
1/4 cup unsalted butter
1 tablespoon peeled and minced fresh ginger
1/8 teaspoon ground nutmeg
2 tablespoons pure maple syrup
2 tablespoons chopped pecans

After soaking the millet overnight, drain the water and transfer the millet to a medium saucepan. Add the 2 1/2 cups water and the 1/4 teaspoon salt. Bring the millet to a boil, then lower the heat, cover, and cook until dry and fluffy, 15 to 25 minutes.

Meanwhile, preheat the oven to 375°F. Make a small slit in the side of each squash where you will eventually cut the squash in half. Place the squash on an oiled pan and bake until soft but firm, 45 minutes to 1 hour. Remove the squash from the oven (but leave the oven on) and let the squash cool until you can handle them comfortably. Carefully cut each squash in half and scoop out the seeds. An alternative method is to cut the squash before baking. This method requires a sharp and sturdy knife and a sure hand. Cut each squash in half, scoop out the seeds, and place the cut side down on an oiled baking pan. Proceed as described above. With this method the squash will cook somewhat more quickly, 35 to 50 minutes.

In a heavy skillet over medium-high heat, sauté the onion in the 2 tablespoons butter until the onion is sweet and golden brown. Add the turmeric, cumin seed, and klonji. Cook until the cumin is fragrant, a few minutes more. Add the chile and celery and sauté only until they turn bright green.

Mix these spiced onions with the cooked millet and add salt to taste. Stir in the 1/4 cup pecans and parsley. Set aside.

Melt the 1/4 cup butter in a small saucepan. Add the fresh ginger and nutmeg. Cook until the ginger is lightly colored. Remove from the heat and add the maple syrup.

Preheat the oven to 375°F.

To assemble the stuffed squash, place the cooked squash cut side up on an oiled baking pan. Prick the flesh of the squash 1/4 to 1/2 inch deep. Drizzle the ginger butter evenly over the squash.

Fill the squash with the millet pilaf, mounding it firmly and leaving a ring of squash showing. Top with the 2 tablespoons pecans and bake until the squash is hot and the top of the stuffing is golden brown, 10 to 15 minutes.

Serves 4.

Note: Klonji is onion seed. It may be purchased at East Indian grocery stores or natural foods markets. If you can't get it, don't despair; simply add a little more spice to the filling, if desired.

Mushroom Stroganoff

▼▼▼▼▼▼▼▼▼▼▼▼▼

Stroganoff is one of those old-fashioned creamy and comforting foods that makes a warming meal on a cold winter day. I serve this vegetarian version with steamed green, red, and yellow vegetables.

1 tablespoon extravirgin olive oil
1 large yellow or white onion, finely sliced
1/2 teaspoon salt
1 pound mushrooms, sliced
1/4 to 1/2 teaspoon black pepper
1/8 teaspoon cayenne pepper
1 tablespoon soy sauce
1/4 teaspoon dried thyme
1/2 teaspoon dried basil
1/4 cup dry sherry or red wine
3 cups sour cream
2 tablespoons minced parsley
1 tablespoon minced fresh tarragon,
or 1 teaspoon dried tarragon
3/4 teaspoon salt, or to taste
1/4 teaspoon salt
8 to 10 ounces dried fettuccine,
or 12 to 14 ounces fresh fettuccine
1 teaspoon minced parsley, for garnish

Heat a medium cast iron or heavy enameled saucepan over high heat. Add the olive oil and saute the onion until barely wilted, about 2 minutes. Add the 1/2 teaspoon salt, mushrooms, black pepper, cayenne, and soy sauce. Continue cooking over high heat, stirring occasionally, until the liquid is gone from the mushrooms and they are seared to a medium brown. This searing creates the rich flavor of the sauce.

Reduce the heat to medium and add the thyme, basil, and sherry. Simmer until the sherry is almost gone, 5 to 10 minutes.

Remove from the heat and stir in the sour cream, the 2 tablespoons parsley, tarragon, and the 3/4 teaspoon salt. Immediately before serving, heat the sauce until steaming (do not boil or the sauce may curdle).

Meanwhile, bring a large pot of water to a boil. Add the 1/4 teaspoon salt. Add the fettuccine and cook until al dente. Drain the pasta in a colander. If you are serving it immediately, it is not necessary to rinse the pasta.

Transfer the pasta to warmed plates. Top with the mushroom mixture, garnish with the 1 teaspoon parsley, and serve immediately.

Serves 4.

Pasta with Roasted Red Pepper Sauce

▼▼▼▼▼▼▼▼▼▼▼▼▼▼

Roasting peppers can be viewed as a simple process or an alchemic mystery. Although we sometimes flame-roast ours for various preparations, we have had very good results using an ordinary oven.

Accompany this pasta dish with hot garlic bread and freshly steamed romano beans and yellow wax beans.

2 large red bell peppers, cored, halved, and seeded
1 small yellow onion, quartered, with layers separated
2 to 3 garlic cloves
3 ripe plum tomatoes,
or 2 ripe medium tomatoes, cored and peeled, if desired
1 to 2 tablespoons extravirgin olive oil
1/8 teaspoon black pepper
1/8 teaspoon white pepper
1/8 teaspoon crushed red chile (chile piquin), optional
1/8 teaspoon paprika
1/2 teaspoon minced fresh oregano,
or 1/8 teaspoon dried oregano
1/4 teaspoon salt, or to taste
1 tablespoon extravirgin olive oil,
or unsalted butter, optional
1 teaspoon balsamic vinegar, optional
1/4 teaspoon salt
8 to 10 ounces dried pasta, preferably spaghetti or linguine,
or 12 to 14 ounces fresh pasta
1/4 cup grated Asiago or Parmesan cheese, for garnish

Preheat the oven to 375°F.

Place the red bell peppers in a dry baking pan, skin side up. Place the onion, garlic, and tomatoes in another dry baking pan. Sprinkle the vegetables with the olive oil.

Place the pan with the peppers on a shelf near the top of the oven. Place the other pan in the middle of the oven. Roast the vegetables until the onion and tomatoes are golden and soft and the skins of the peppers begin to blister and blacken, 15 to 25 minutes. The tomatoes, garlic, and onion may be done before the peppers.

Remove the pans to wire racks. Immediately transfer the roasted bell peppers to a small glass or stainless steel bowl, cover with a tight-fitting lid or plastic wrap, and allow to steam for 10 minutes. This will loosen the skins and make peeling them very easy.

Peel the bell peppers and place them in a blender container. Add the roasted tomatoes, garlic, and onion. Add all the spices, the 1 tablespoon olive oil, and the vinegar, if desired. Blend until smooth. You may need to add a small amount of water or stock to thin the sauce. Transfer the sauce to a medium saucepan and heat gently. Cover and keep warm.

Bring a large pot of water to a boil. Add 1/4 teaspoon salt. Add the pasta and cook until al dente. Drain the pasta in a colander. If serving immediately, it is not necessary to rinse the pasta.

Transfer the pasta to warmed plates. Top with the Roasted Red Pepper Sauce, garnish with the grated cheese, and serve immediately.

Serves 4.

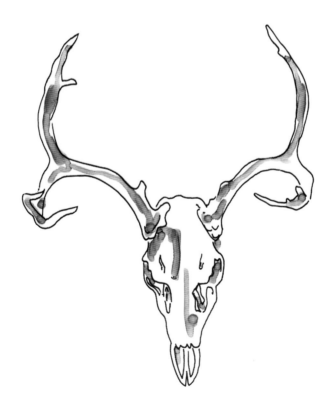

East Indian Potato Pancakes
with Cucumber Raita

▼▼▼▼▼▼▼▼▼▼▼▼▼▼▼▼

Many people are familiar with the Eastern European potato latkes, but this spicy East Indian version may be thought unusual. The idea was suggested by my friend Mr. Kashyap, but I am sure that it has been westernized in our kitchen. Serve the pancakes with Cucumber Raita for a light meal.

3 large white potatoes, peeled if desired,
grated into cold water to cover
1 medium white or yellow onion, grated
1 1/3 teaspoons cumin seed
1/2 teaspoon ground turmeric
2 tablespoons light sesame oil
2 teaspoons ground coriander
1 small hot green chile (jalapeño), seeded and minced
1/3 teaspoon ground New Mexico red chile,
or 1/8 teaspoon cayenne pepper
1/4 teaspoon black pepper
1/3 cup finely sliced green onion
1/3 cup minced cilantro
1 1/4 teaspoons salt
1/4 cup unbleached white flour
1 egg, beaten
2 to 4 tablespoons sesame
or light vegetable oil, for frying

Drain the grated potato and add the grated onion. In a small saucepan or skillet, toast the cumin seed and turmeric in the sesame oil until the cumin is fragrant. Add to the potato and onion mixture.

Add the coriander, green chile, red chile, black pepper, green onion, cilantro, salt, flour, and egg. Stir well or mix with your hands. Cover and let stand 15 to 20 minutes.

Warm a large griddle or skillet over medium-high heat. Add only enough sesame oil to coat the bottom of the pan. Scoop up approximately 3 tablespoons of the mixture with your hand or a spoon. Place on the hot griddle and flatten out to about a 4-inch circle. This is actually easiest to do with your hands, but you must be careful to pat only the pancake.

Fry the pancakes until they are golden brown, 2 to 4 minutes on each side. Serve them immediately with the Cucumber Raita on the side. If necessary, drain the pancakes on paper towels and refry them briefly in a little oil right before serving.

Makes fifteen 4-inch pancakes; serves 5.

Cucumber Raita

1 1/2 cups plain yogurt
1 small cucumber, peeled and grated (see Note)
1 teaspoon ground cumin
1/2 teaspoon minced cilantro
2 teaspoons minced mint, optional
1/2 teaspoon salt

Whisk the yogurt, then add the remaining ingredients. Stir well and chill. That's it!

Makes approximately 2 cups.

Note: Make sure to cut off the ends of the cucumber, since they are almost always bitter. Then taste the remaining flesh to make sure that it is not bitter, which would ruin the raita.

Masala Dosas with Two Chutneys

▼▼▼▼▼▼▼▼▼▼▼▼▼▼▼

Dosas are one of those Eastern foods that seem like a miracle. They are as light as French crepes (though with a much more pronounced flavor), but are pancakes made from very simple ingredients—rice and dal.

In India, dosas are primarily enjoyed for breakfast or as a snack. I serve them for lunch or dinner stuffed with Coriander Chutney and Red or Green Chile Potatoes, topped with Tamarind Chutney, and accompanied by plain yogurt or Cucumber Raita (see page 71).

This dish does take planning, since the rice and dal for the dosas need to be soaked and the potatoes need to be boiled and allowed to cool before baking.

Dosas

1/2 cup washed urad dal (see Note)
1 cup white or brown rice (not basmati or sweet rice)
Water to cover dal and rice for soaking
2 1/2 cups water
3/4 teaspoon salt
1 small hot green chile (jalapeño),
seeded and minced, optional
3 to 5 tablespoons light sesame oil
2 tablespoons cilantro leaves, for garnish

Place the dal and rice in a medium bowl and wash with cool water until the water becomes clear. Drain again, cover with clean water, and soak overnight in a cool place but not in the refrigerator. In the morning, drain the mixture through a fine sieve.

Place the drained dal and rice in a blender container. Add the 2 1/2 cups water and the salt. Blend on high speed until smooth.

Pour the batter into a large bowl and let stand in a warm place until slightly foamy and risen, 3 to 6 hours. The fermentation that causes the rising is what gives the dosas their light texture and slightly tart flavor. If allowed to stand too long, however, the batter may become too sour. Before cooking the dosas, add the chile, if desired.

To cook the dosas, use a griddle, cast iron frying pan, or crepe pan. Using 2 or 3 pans will make the process go faster. Heat the pan thoroughly over medium-high heat, add 1 teaspoon sesame oil, and distribute it to cover an 8-inch area. Immediately ladle 1/3 cup of the batter onto the pan. Spread the batter lightly but quickly, using the back of the ladle to smooth the batter in outward spirals from the center to the edge of the dosa. This will take some practice to do easily, but it is not a difficult maneuver. (If you want a thinner dosa, add 1 tablespoon water at a time to the batter until you reach the desired consistency.)

Cook the dosa until the top appears dry, 1 to 2 minutes. Turn the dosa and cook on the other side until the bottom is golden. Remove from the pan and cover until serving. Repeat this process until all of the batter has been used.

To assemble the stuffed dosas, heat each dosa on the griddle, spread 1/2 to 1 teaspoon Coriander Chutney (recipe follows) on half of the dosa, and place about 3 tablespoons Red or Green Chile Potatoes (recipe follows) on top of the chutney. Fold in half and top with a line of Tamarind Chutney (recipe follows) or a spicy lentil sauce. Garnish with cilantro leaves and serve. Serve 2 stuffed dosas per person.

Serves 6.

Note: Dal is the Indian name for lentils. Urad dal is the hulled and split black gram bean, which is ivory in color. It may be found in East Indian grocery stores.

Red or Green Chile Potatoes
(filling for dosas)

3 pounds white potatoes (approximately 6 large potatoes)
Water to cover potatoes
2 medium yellow or white onions, finely diced
2 tablespoons light sesame oil
4 teaspoons cumin seed
3/4 teaspoon ground turmeric
1/2 teaspoon salt
2 tablespoons ground New Mexico red chile,
or 2 small hot green chiles (jalapeño), seeded and minced
3 to 4 tablespoons light sesame oil

1 teaspoon salt, or to taste
1/2 teaspoon black pepper
1/4 cup minced cilantro

Wash the potatoes and place them in a large saucepan. Add the water and bring to a boil, then reduce the heat and simmer the potatoes until they are cooked but still firm. Drain the potatoes and let cool in cold water. Peel the potatoes and dice into 5/8-inch cubes. Set aside.

In a heavy skillet over medium-high heat, sauté the onions in the 2 tablespoons oil until golden. Add the cumin seed, turmeric, and the 1/2 teaspoon salt. Continue to cook until the cumin is fragrant and the onions are very sweet, stirring often. Add the chile and cook 1 more minute. Remove the pan from the heat and set aside.

Preheat the oven to 425°F. Place the cubed potatoes in an oiled baking pan so that they are one layer deep. Sprinkle on the 3 to 4 tablespoons reserved oil, the 1 teaspoon salt, and black pepper. Bake the potatoes until golden brown and crispy, approximately 10 minutes.

Toss the potatoes with the sautéed onion mixture. Add the cilantro, and taste for salt. Potatoes need salt to bring out their delicate flavor. If desired, you may add a small amount of water just before serving.

Serves 6.

Coriander Chutney

1/4 cup packed cilantro leaves
2 tablespoons unsweetened shredded coconut
1 clove garlic, pressed or minced
1/2 teaspoon peeled and minced fresh ginger
1/4 cup sliced green onion
1/2 to 1 small hot green chile (jalapeño),
seeded and minced
2 tablespoons lemon juice
1/8 teaspoon salt

Place all the ingredients in the bowl of a food processor or a blender container. Process until well mixed. If using a blender, it may be necessary to add several tablespoons of water to the chutney so that the ingredients blend thoroughly.

This chutney is best used the day it is made.
Makes approximately 1/2 cup.

Tamarind Chutney

1 teaspoon pressed garlic
2 teaspoons peeled and grated fresh ginger
1/2 teaspoon light sesame oil
1/4 cup plus 1 tablespoon tamarind concentrate (see Note)
1/2 cup hot water
3 to 4 tablespoons pure maple syrup
1/8 teaspoon cayenne pepper
1/8 teaspoon salt
1 teaspoon kuzu (See note)
1/4 cup water

In a small saucepan over medium heat, sauté the garlic and ginger in the oil until fragrant.

Mix together the tamarind and the hot water and add to the pan. Add the maple syrup, cayenne, and salt and simmer for 5 minutes.

Dissolve the kuzu in the 1/4 cup water and stir into the tamarind mixture. Bring to a boil and simmer only until the chutney becomes translucent and thickened.

This chutney will keep, covered in the refrigerator, for several weeks.
Makes 1/2 cup.

Note: Tamarind trees, which are large and graceful, grow in tropical places. They bear a fruit that is often used in sweetened beverages. The concentrate can be purchased in jars from East Indian grocery stores.

Kuzu is a root that is a stable thickener. It is also reputed to aid digestion. Arrowroot or cornstarch may be substituted if necessary. Kuzu can be purchased in the Asian food section of most natural foods grocery stores.

Tempeh Curry with Potato Chapatis
▼▼▼▼▼▼▼▼▼▼▼▼▼▼▼

This recipe was given to me by an especially talented East Indian cook and storyteller. Serve the curry, rice, and chapatis with steamed cauliflower and greens.

Creamy Curry Sauce

2 tablespoons peeled and minced or grated fresh ginger
5 cloves garlic, minced or pressed
2 tablespoons light sesame oil
1 large or 2 small yellow
or white onions, diced (see Note)
1 teaspoon whole black peppercorns
1/4 teaspoon ground turmeric
5 ripe tomatoes, cored and diced
1/2 to 1 small hot green chile (jalapeño), seeded and minced
1/4 teaspoon salt
2 teaspoons poppy seeds
2 teaspoons ground cumin
1 teaspoon ground coriander
1 teaspoon curry powder
1/8 teaspoon cayenne pepper
1/2 cup water
1/8 teaspoon ground cloves
1/8 teaspoon ground cinnamon
1 cup whipping cream
1 1/4 teaspoons salt, or to taste
3 tablespoons minced cilantro

Over medium-high heat, sauté the ginger and garlic in the sesame oil until fragrant, 1 to 2 minutes. Add the diced onion, peppercorns, and turmeric and sauté until medium brown and very sweet. Stir frequently. Add the tomatoes, green chile, and the 1/4 teaspoon salt. Reduce the heat to medium and cook until the vegetables are soft, 10 to 20 minutes. Add the poppy seeds, cumin, coriander, curry powder, and cayenne. Stir well and cook for another 2 to 3 minutes.

Transfer the cooked vegetables to a blender container, add the 1/2 cup water, and blend until smooth. Stir in the cloves, cinnamon, whipping cream, the 1 1/4 teaspoons salt, and cilantro. Taste for salt and spice. Heat briefly before serving. Do not boil.

Serve hot over Grilled Tempeh and Basmati Rice, accompanied by the Potato Chapatis (recipes follow).

Serves 6.

Note: If you do not want to use a blender, simply mince the onion and finely dice the tomatoes before cooking. This will not yield a smooth sauce, but it will be beautiful and very tasty.

Chicken Curry Variation: Marinate 1 3/4 pounds boneless, skinless chicken pieces in the 2 teaspoons cumin, the 1 teaspoon coriander, and 2 teaspoons lemon juice for 1 hour. Meanwhile, prepare the Creamy Curry Sauce, omitting the cumin and coriander. Sauté the marinated chicken in 2 to 3 tablespoons light sesame oil until lightly browned and tender. Add to the sauce. Taste for salt and spice, most likely adding an additional 1/2 teaspoon salt and 1/8 teaspoon cayenne pepper. Simmer over low heat only until the flavors meld. Serve over Basmati Rice accompanied by Potato Chapatis.

Grilled Tempeh

12 ounces tempeh (see Note)
2 teaspoons lemon juice
1 to 2 tablespoons light sesame oil

Cut the tempeh into thin strips, approximately 1/8 inch by 2 inches by 1/2 inch (the thickness of the tempeh). Sprinkle the lemon juice over the tempeh and marinate for 1 hour. Over medium-high heat, sauté the tempeh in the sesame oil until golden brown and crisp on each side, 6 to 10 minutes.

Serves 6.

Note: Tempeh is a traditional Indonesian soy food that is easily digested. It is available in many bean and grain combinations. Soy-rice tempeh is the variety that we use primarily, since it becomes nice and crispy. Tempeh is available in most natural foods stores.

Basmati Rice

1 1/2 cups basmati rice
3 cups water
1/2 teaspoon salt
2 tablespoons unsalted butter

Wash the rice thoroughly in cool water until the water becomes clear. Drain and set aside. In a medium saucepan bring the water to a boil with the salt. Add the rice and return to a boil. Add the butter, reduce the heat to low, cover, and cook until the water is gone and the rice is fluffy, approximately 20 minutes. Keep the pot covered an additional 15 minutes before serving. This resting period is necessary for the grains of rice to completely absorb the moisture and retain their shape when stirred.
Serves 6.

Potato Chapatis

This chapati recipe also appears in <u>Santa Fe Lite and Spicy Recipe</u> from Tierra Publications, Joan Stromquist, editor.

3 large white potatoes, washed
Water to cover potatoes
2 tablespoons light sesame oil
1 teaspoon salt
1/2 to 1 teaspoon toasted cumin seed, optional
1 cup whole wheat pastry flour
1/2 cup unbleached white flour
1/2 cup whole wheat bread flour
Light sesame oil for bowl and chapati dough
1/4 cup ghee (see page 87)
or unsalted butter, melted
Unbleached white flour, for rolling chapatis

Place the potatoes in a medium saucepan, cover with the water, bring to a boil, and cook until very tender. Drain and let cool in water. When the potatoes are cool enough to handle comfortably, peel them and mash well. Add the sesame oil, salt, and cumin seed, if desired. Slowly add the three flours, mixing well with your hands, until the dough is soft and barely sticky. You may not need all of the flour, depending on the size and moisture content of the potatoes. Place the chapati dough in an oiled medium bowl, oil the top of the dough, cover, and let stand for 2 hours.

Divide the dough into 12 pieces and shape them into balls. On a lightly floured board, gently roll out each chapati until it is 1/16 inch thick. The more evenly you roll, the more round your chapatis will be.

Heat a seasoned griddle or large cast iron skillet over medium heat until it is hot. Cook each chapati on one side until it is slightly puffed and golden brown, 1 to 2 minutes. Brush the chapati with the melted ghee and flip it over to cook the other side. Brush the cooked side with ghee and cook another 1 to 2 minutes.

Remove each chapati to a board covered with a tea towel. As the chapatis stack up, keep them covered with the towel. Serve the chapatis warm, if possible, although they are delicious at any temperature.

Serves 6.

Fresh Salmon au Poivre

▼▼▼▼▼▼▼▼▼▼▼▼▼▼

Freshness is essential for a wonderful fish dinner. Even here in the desert, fish are now flown in daily from the rivers and oceans. Farm-raised fish, too, arrive by air, and are often, in these days of polluted waters, a very good choice, both for purity and freshness.

If you haven't caught the fish yourself, I recommend buying it from someone you can really trust, and examining it carefully before you take it home. With whole fish, the eyes should be bright, not cloudy, and the flesh should be firm. In buying fillets, look for a beautiful pearly translucence of the flesh. The fish should smell fresh and clean, not "fishy."

Take the fish home immediately, rinse it briefly in cold water, pat dry, place on a rack in a shallow pan, and cover with ice. It is important that the fish not sit in water, so if you don't have a pan with a rack, just place the clean, dry fillets in a plastic bag, seal it well, and lay the enclosed fish in a pan. Again, cover with ice. If the fish is very fresh, you can store it this way in the refrigerator for up to 2 days, although it is best eaten as soon as possible.

This dish is a variation of steak au poivre. The salmon has a delicate strength that stands up well to the pepper. Cook the fish to your taste, but the key to cooking a delicious fish dish is not to overcook it. A good guideline is to look for a thin line of translucence in the center of the fish, which is your cue to remove the fish from the heat and serve immediately.

Four 8-ounce fresh salmon fillets
(Atlantic, King, or Sockeye), 1/2 to 3/4 inch thick
1 to 2 tablespoons freshly cracked black pepper (see Note)
2 tablespoons unsalted butter
Juice of 1 lime
Pinch salt
1 lime, seeded and cut into quarters, for garnish

Rinse the salmon fillets in very cold water, drain, and pat dry. Sprinkle the cracked pepper on both sides of the fish, pressing it in lightly.

Heat a large cast iron or other heavy skillet over medium-high heat. Melt the butter and immediately add the peppered salmon. Cook the fish until the sides look just opaque, 3 to 5 minutes. Turn the fillets, sprinkle with the lime juice and salt, and continue cooking until the fish is done to your taste, another 3 to 5 minutes. If you are not experienced at cooking fish, it is better to peek inside one of the fillets with a sharp knife than to overcook it.

Garnish with the lime wedges and serve immediately.

Serves 4.

Note: It is very easy to crack peppercorns with a mortar and pestle. If this is not possible, you can use an adjustable pepper mill set to grind coarsely. Or to prepare a larger amount, grind the pepper briefly in a spice mill or blender. You may wish to try green or pink peppercorns for varied flavor and color.

Fresh Tuna Teriyaki

▼▼▼▼▼▼▼▼▼▼▼▼▼▼

Yellowfin tuna that is very fresh is best for this dish. We often use "sushi grade" tuna, but that isn't necessary as long as the fish is firm, translucent, and reddish in color (not a dull brown).

Serve the tuna simply with rice and colorful steamed vegetables.

1/4 cup soy sauce
2 tablespoons sake or white wine
1 to 2 tablespoons pure maple syrup
1 teaspoon ginger juice (see page 7)
1/4 teaspoon apple cider vinegar,
or rice wine vinegar
1 to 2 cloves garlic, pressed
Pinch cayenne pepper
Pinch salt
Four 8-ounce fresh tuna steaks, 1/2 to 3/4 inch thick
1 to 2 tablespoons light sesame oil
1 lemon, quartered
2 tablespoons very finely sliced green onion, for garnish

Mix together the soy sauce, sake, maple syrup, ginger juice, vinegar, garlic, cayenne, and salt. Marinate the tuna for 5 minutes (longer will tend to make the flavor too strong, as well as starting to "cook" the fish, as with ceviche).

Heat a large, heavy skillet over medium-high heat. Sprinkle the sesame oil into the skillet and immediately place the tuna steaks in the pan. Reserve the remaining marinade.

Cook only until the edges of the fish begin to look opaque, 3 to 4 minutes. Turn the fish, squeeze the lemon onto the fish, and pour the remaining marinade over all. Cook only until the tuna is still pink inside but lightly browned on the outside, a few minutes more.

Remove the fish to warm serving plates. Immediately increase the heat under the skillet to high and cook only long enough to thicken the remaining sauce. Pour it in a line over each piece of fish. Garnish with the green onion and serve immediately.

Serves 4.

Red Chile Lemon Chicken

▼▼▼▼▼▼▼▼▼▼▼▼▼▼▼

Here is a spicy and tasty chicken dish that is wonderful with a summer salad and cornbread or grilled polenta. Summer or winter squash also accompany the chicken nicely.

Four 8-ounce boneless, skinless chicken breasts
1/3 cup lemon juice
1 teaspoon grated lemon zest
1/2 teaspoon pressed or minced garlic
1/2 teaspoon paprika
1/2 teaspoon ground New Mexico red chile
1/2 teaspoon crushed red chile (chile piquin)
1/4 teaspoon black pepper
2 tablespoons light sesame oil
1 tablespoon honey
1/8 teaspoon salt

Wash the chicken in cold water, drain, pat dry, and reserve.

Mix together all the other ingredients. Place the chicken in this marinade and coat well. Cover and marinate in the refrigerator for 3 to 4 hours.

Grill or broil the chicken until it is tender but no longer pink inside, 3 to 5 minutes on each side. Serve immediately.

Serves 4.

Grilled Chicken with Mango Salsa
or Cranberry Glaze

▼▼▼▼▼▼▼▼▼▼▼▼▼

These simple dishes are both light and flavorful and go very well paired with a good Gewürztraminer. Accompany the Mango Salsa version with basmati rice and sautéed greens; serve the cranberry-glazed chicken with wild rice and mixed vegetables.

Prepare either sauce before you grill the chicken.

Grilled Chicken

Four 8-ounce skinless, boneless chicken breasts
2 tablespoons light sesame oil
1 tablespoon lemon juice
1/4 teaspoon black pepper
Pinch salt

Wash the chicken in cold water, drain well, and pat dry. Mix together the sesame oil, lemon juice, pepper, and salt. Drizzle the oil mixture over the chicken and rub it well to coat the chicken completely. Let stand for 15 minutes.

Grill or broil the marinated chicken breasts until tender but no longer pink inside, approximately 4 minutes on each side.

Top the chicken with the Mango Salsa or the Cranberry Glaze and serve immediately.

Serves 4.

Mango Salsa

1 firm ripe mango, peeled, seeded, and finely diced
2 tablespoons lemon juice
1 tablespoon lime juice
2 teaspoons minced green onion
1 small hot green chile (jalapeño), seeded and minced
1 tablespoon minced cilantro
1/4 teaspoon salt
1/4 teaspoon crushed red chile (chile piquin)

For the best visual appeal, dice the mango evenly. Stir all the ingredients together. Serve at room temperature.

If you need to prepare the salsa ahead, you may mix all of the ingredients except the cilantro and green onion and keep covered in the refrigerator for 1 day.

Makes approximately 1/2 cup.

Cranberry Glaze

3/4 cup dry red wine
6 ounces fresh cranberries
2 tablespoons honey
1/8 teaspoon salt
2 tablespoons water, if needed

In a small saucepan over medium heat, reduce the wine to half its volume. Add the cranberries and cook only until the berries pop.

Add the honey and salt, and the water to thin if needed.

This glaze will keep well, covered in the refrigerator, for several days.

Makes approximately 1/2 cup.

Grilled "Tandoori" Chicken
▼▼▼▼▼▼▼▼▼▼▼▼▼▼

A tandoor is an East Indian clay oven that is used to roast meats and bake breads at very high temperatures. This chicken recipe is my "gringo" version of the famous Tandoori chicken made in many fine Indian restaurants. Serve the chicken with basmati rice and a plain or spicy vegetable dish, such as Sugar Snap Peas with Mint Raita (page 28) or Sesame Carrots and Jerusalem Artichokes (page 29). Although this is a simple dish to prepare, you will need to plan ahead, since the chicken must marinate for 8 to 24 hours.

2 pounds skinless chicken pieces
(legs, thighs, and/or breasts)
3 cloves garlic, pressed
1 tablespoon peeled and minced,
or grated fresh ginger
1 teaspoon ground coriander
3/4 teaspoon ground cumin
1/2 teaspoon ground turmeric
1/4 teaspoon ground cloves
1/2 teaspoon ground cardamom
1/2 teaspoon cayenne pepper
1/4 teaspoon black pepper
1 1/2 teaspoons paprika
1 teaspoon salt
2 tablespoons lemon juice
2 tablespoons light sesame oil
1/4 cup plain yogurt
Ghee, for basting, optional (see Note)
1 white onion, sliced paper thin, for garnish
1 lemon, quartered, for garnish

Wash the chicken pieces in cold water, drain, and pat dry. Make 1/4-inch-deep slits 1 inch apart in the chicken. This will help the marinade to penetrate.

In a medium bowl mix together all the other ingredients except the ghee and garnishes. Add the chicken pieces and mix with your hands to coat the chicken with the marinade. Cover and refrigerate for 8 to 24 hours.

If desired, drizzle ghee on the marinated chicken before cooking. Grill or broil the chicken over high heat until tender but no longer pink inside, approximately 5 minutes on each side. You may want to baste with ghee when you turn the chicken pieces.

Garnish with the onion slices and serve with the lemon wedges, squeezing the juice over the hot chicken at the table.

Serves 4.

Note: Ghee is East Indian clarified butter. The simplest way I have found to make it is to melt the butter (1 pound will yield approximately 1 1/2 cups) over low heat and simmer it until the foam disappears and the milk solids at the bottom of the pan congeal but are not browned. The key is to keep the heat quite low and watch patiently. Let the butter cool slightly, then pour off the clear liquid into a jar. If poured carefully, you should not have to strain the ghee, but it can be strained through a double layer of cheesecloth if necessary. The ghee will keep at room temperature, but I like to keep it covered in the refrigerator for maximum freshness.

Grilled Rosemary Chicken

▼▼▼▼▼▼▼▼▼▼▼▼▼

Chicken is wonderful for a summer barbecue. This dish may also be cooked under an oven broiler.

Four 8- to 10-ounce boneless,
skinless chicken breasts
1/3 cup finely chopped fresh rosemary
1/3 cup dry white wine
1/3 cup extravirgin olive oil
3/4 teaspoon black pepper
2 to 3 cloves garlic, pressed
1 1/2 tablespoons minced green onion
1/4 to 1/2 teaspoon salt

Rinse the chicken in cold water, drain well, and pat dry.

Mix together all the remaining ingredients. Add the chicken breasts to the marinade; cover and refrigerate for 1 to 4 hours.

Grill or broil the chicken until tender, about 3 to 5 minutes on each side. Brush the chicken with the marinade at least once during cooking. Serve hot.

Serves 4.

Desserts

D esserts inspire such a range of feelings in most of us: anticipation, delight, guilt. I have always loved sweets and have mostly felt guilty about that desire. Some years ago a good friend often took me out for ice cream breaks during fourteen-hour workdays at the restaurant. He always encouraged me to thoroughly enjoy the ice cream, and I came to see that if you aren't plagued by the guilt, you can eat less of something that you desire and completely experience and enjoy it. Therein comes appreciation instead of craving.

When you make these desserts for your family and friends, enjoy them to the fullest. They are all quite simple to put together. Some are very rich and some are light; all are delicious.

A few notes on preparation: It is useful to assemble all the ingredients required in a recipe before you begin cooking. Then, when you have finished, the counter will be empty!

Although it is convenient to use an electric mixer to beat egg whites and whipping cream, and an electric blender is useful for several of the recipes, all of these desserts can be made without the use of electric appliances.

There are no directions for sifting ingredients because sifting is not needed in these recipes. Simply whisk the dry ingredients to aerate and mix them. This will ensure even absorption when the liquids are added.

If you have never used whole wheat pastry flour, you will discover a wonderful ingredient through these recipes. Whole wheat pastry flour is made from soft white wheat, which is high in starch and low in gluten. It has the nutty flavor of whole wheat flour and gives the tender texture of cake flour.

Maple syrup and honey are not interchangeable. Maple syrup is a wonderful sweetener to make delicate cakes and combines very well with chocolate. I primarily like to use honey with fruits, where its strong flavor will be balanced and perceived as an asset.

Please use pure vanilla extract only. Artificial flavoring is not worth the small financial saving. When eggs are called for, use large eggs.

Know your oven. Keep an accurate thermometer in it and check it often. If you know that there are hot spots, you can compensate for them. In ignorance, there is no bliss.

There are many fine baking books available that discuss technique in detail. Please refer to them and use your experience as a guide in making these desserts. I have always found that success in baking comes from allowing intuition to take over once the ingredients have been properly measured. Use all of your senses and you will have spectacular results.

Fresh Mango Mousse

▼▼▼▼▼▼▼▼▼▼▼▼▼▼

Mango fool is the basis for this recipe. I began with complicated custards that had to be cooked and cooled. Then, one day after making a mango shake at home (mango, milk, vanilla ice cream, and a pinch of cardamom, blended smooth) I thought: simplicity is often best, and tastiest. So, here is a simply wonderful version of a mango mousse.

3 or 4 large ripe mangoes,
pitted and peeled
1/2 cup whipping cream
1/4 teaspoon almond extract
2 tablespoons pure maple syrup

Chill a small bowl and electric beaters in the freezer.

Purée the mango pulp in a blender, then strain through a fine sieve into a small bowl. Ladle 1 teaspoon of the puree into the bottom of each of five 5-ounce dessert glasses.

In the chilled bowl with the chilled beaters, whip the cream, almond extract, and maple syrup to medium peaks. Gently fold this mixture into the remaining mango purée. Ladle the mousse into the glasses and chill before serving.

Serve this dessert the day it is made, or, if necessary, cover and refrigerate for up to 1 day. It will soften slightly.

Serves 5.

Key Lime Mousse

▼▼▼▼▼▼▼▼▼▼▼▼▼▼▼

This refreshing but rich dessert is a sister to the famous Florida Key lime pie. It is good on its own, or can be dressed up with a topping of fresh berries.

2 1/2 cups whipping cream
2 egg yolks
1/4 cup honey
1/8 teaspoon vanilla extract
1/4 cup Key lime juice
1/2 teaspoon grated lime zest, for garnish

In a small saucepan over low heat, simmer the cream approximately 1 hour, reducing the volume to 1 3/4 cups. Stir occasionally.

Whisk together the egg yolks, honey, and vanilla in a small nonreactive bowl. Slowly pour the hot cream into the egg and honey mixture, whisking constantly. Let cool completely, then chill before proceeding. The mousse may be prepared up to this point one day ahead of serving.

Slowly beat in the Key lime juice with an electric mixer, or whisk vigorously by hand until the mousse becomes lighter in color and begins to thicken. It will momentarily thin after the lime juice is added, but do not be concerned. After the mixture thickens, continue to beat for 2 more minutes.

Spoon the mousse into 6-ounce dessert glasses and garnish with grated lime zest. Chill at least 1 hour before serving. The mousse will keep up to 3 days refrigerated.

Serves 5.

Raspberry Kanten

▼▼▼▼▼▼▼▼▼▼▼▼▼

This dessert is delicious and fat-free, yet the only way to accurately describe it is as a natural fruit "Jello," which conjures up memories of rubbery lime green concoctions. However, people really enjoy it.

4 cups fresh raspberries, rinsed and sorted
2 1/2 cups apple juice
1 1/2 tablespoons agar-agar flakes (see Note)
2 tablespoons honey

Arrange 3 cups of the berries in six 6-ounce dessert glasses. Set aside.

In a small nonreactive saucepan, bring the apple juice, agar-agar flakes, and the remaining cup berries to a boil. Reduce the heat and simmer until the agar-agar has dissolved completely, approximately 10 minutes.

Remove the pan from the heat. Strain the juice through a fine sieve; add the honey and let cool for 5 to 10 minutes. Agar-agar will set at room temperature, so don't allow the juice to cool for too long.

Pour the juice over the berries, making sure that all of the fruit is covered. Chill and serve.

The kanten will keep up to 2 days covered and refrigerated.

Serves 6.

Note: Agar-agar, or kanten, is a sea vegetable that is virtually tasteless and can be used similarly to animal gelatin. It is necessary, however, to dissolve it by cooking in a hot liquid. Agar-agar flakes can be purchased at most natural foods stores.

Blueberry Kanten Variation: Substitute fresh blueberries for the raspberries. Arrange 3 1/2 cups of the berries in the glasses, and use the remaining 1/2 cup blueberries to cook with the apple juice and agar-agar.

Kheer

▼▼▼▼▼▼▼▼▼▼▼▼▼

My friends from India introduced me to this delicate rice pudding It is thickened by the starch in the rice as well as the reduction of the milk. Be sure to use the large pan recommended, because the milk will rise up considerably when first brought to a boil. Gently blow on the foaming milk to reduce its volume.

1/4 cup Indian basmati rice (see Note)
3 cups whole milk
1 tablespoon unsalted butter
2 threads saffron, optional
1/3 cup whole cashew nuts
2 tablespoons currants or raisins, optional
1/4 cup pure maple syrup
1/4 teaspoon ground cardamom
1/4 teaspoon rose water or 1/3 teaspoon grated lemon zest

Wash the rice in cool water until the water runs clear. Bring the rice, milk, butter, and saffron to a boil in a large, heavy saucepan. Boil for 5 minutes, then reduce the heat to low and simmer until the rice is very soft, approximately 40 minutes. Stir the mixture occasionally with a wooden spoon. Too much or too vigorous stirring will break the beautiful grains of rice.

Meanwhile, roast the cashew nuts in a dry pan in a 325°F oven until golden brown, approximately 5 minutes. (A toaster oven works efficiently for this step.) Let the nuts cool, and reserve. Add the currants (if used), maple syrup, and cardamom to the rice and milk mixture. Simmer another 5 minutes. Remove the pan from the heat and stir in the rose water. Let the kheer cool to lukewarm, then stir in 1/4 cup of the toasted cashew nuts. Pour into a serving bowl and chill in the refrigerator. Immediately before serving, top with the remaining 2 tablespoons toasted cashew nuts.

The kheer will thicken as it cools, but it is looser than a western rice pudding that is set with eggs. It will keep up to 2 days, covered in the refrigerator.

Serves 4.

Note: Indian basmati rice is best to use because it will fluff up into soft but separate grains. Thai basmati or texmati rice may be substituted if necessary. Look for Indian basmati rice in an East Indian grocery store or a natural foods market.

Chocolate Pôt de Crème

▼▼▼▼▼▼▼▼▼▼▼▼▼▼

This rich stovetop custard is our answer to an elegant chocolate dessert that is simple to make. Serve topped with whipped cream or a small dollop of vanilla or coffee ice cream.

1 cup half-and-half
1/2 cup whipping cream
3 ounces unsweetened baking chocolate
1/2 cup pure maple syrup
1/3 cup brewed coffee (a good decaf is fine)
1 teaspoon vanilla extract
Pinch ground cinnamon
4 egg yolks, beaten and strained

In a medium heavy-bottomed saucepan over low heat, simmer the half-and-half, whipping cream, and chocolate until smooth, stirring occasionally.

Whisk in the maple syrup and coffee. The mixture will temporarily separate at this point but will soon become smooth again. Gently simmer until the chocolate coats a spoon well, approximately 5 minutes, whisking occasionally.

Stir in the vanilla and cinnamon, then remove the pan from the heat. Immediately pour one quarter of the hot chocolate mixture into the beaten and strained eggs, whisking constantly until smooth.

Immediately return the egg mixture to the hot chocolate in the saucepan and whisk until very smooth. Stir to cool until the steam is gone, approximately 3 minutes.

Pour the finished custard into 4- to 6-ounce dessert cups. Chill before serving. Covered in the refrigerator, the pôt de crèmes will keep up to 4 days.

Serves 4 to 6.

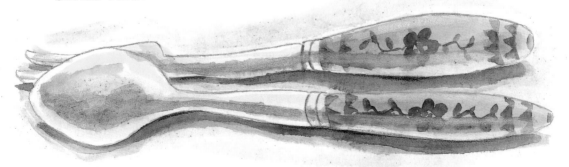

Honey Custard

▼▼▼▼▼▼▼▼▼▼▼▼▼▼

Custards are smooth, creamy, and comforting. This is a rich version of one my mother used to make in handmade stoneware mugs. Any relatively straight-sided 5-ounce ovenproof cups will do nicely.

Serve plain, or top with fresh berries and drizzle with honey.

1 1/2 cups half-and-half, or whole milk
1/3 cup whipping cream
2-inch cinnamon stick
2 whole eggs
2 egg yolks
1/4 cup honey
1/8 teaspoon ground nutmeg
1/2 teaspoon vanilla extract

Preheat the oven to 300°F. Have ready five 5-ounce custard cups and a baking pan in which to set them.

In a medium saucepan over medium heat, scald the half-and-half, cream, and cinnamon stick (see Note). Meanwhile, whisk the eggs and yolks in a small bowl. Add the honey, nutmeg, and vanilla and whisk gently until well blended.

Remove the cinnamon stick from the hot cream mixture. Slowly pour the hot cream into the honey and egg mixture, whisking gently. Strain through a fine sieve and skim off any foam.

Pour the liquid custard mixture into the cups and place them in the baking pan. Add enough hot water to the pan to come halfway up the sides of the custard cups. This will ensure even setting of the custard.

Bake the custards in the bottom third of the oven until barely firm, 30 to 45 minutes. Remove the cups from the pan of water and let cool on a wire rack.

Chill and keep covered in the refrigerator until serving. These custards keep up to 4 days, although they are sure to be eaten before that!

Serves 5.

Note: Scalding milk or cream is bringing it to the temperature just below the boiling point. Tiny bubbles will appear around the edges of the pan, but the milk will not foam. This process is useful in cooking the custards relatively quickly, or to have hot milk for your morning tea or coffee. For ease of cleaning, rinse the pan first with cold water before scalding milk or cream.

English Bread Pudding
with Honey Crème Anglaise

▼▼▼▼▼▼▼▼▼▼▼▼▼▼▼▼

I worked on bread pudding for what seemed like years and was never satisfied. It was either too hard or too soft. Bettina perfected this recipe. It is just right.

English Bread Pudding

Butter, for pan
1 1/2 cups packed coarse dry bread crumbs (see Note)
3/4 cup currants or raisins
1/2 cup dark rum
3 3/4 cups half-and-half or whole milk
1/3 cup unsalted butter
4 eggs, beaten
1/2 cup honey
1 1/2 teaspoons ground cinnamon
1/2 teaspoon ground nutmeg
1 tablespoon dark rum
1/8 teaspoon salt
1/2 cup pecans, chopped

Preheat the oven to 325°F. Butter a nonreactive 8-inch square pan. Sprinkle the bread crumbs evenly into the pan.

In a small nonreactive saucepan, simmer the currants and the 1/2 cup rum until the rum has evaporated, approximately 5 minutes. Sprinkle the warm currants evenly over the bread crumbs.

Heat the half-and-half and butter only until the butter melts. Reserve.

Whisk together the beaten eggs, honey, cinnamon, nutmeg, the 1 tablespoon rum, and salt. Slowly pour the warm half-and-half mixture into the egg mixture. Then pour this evenly over the bread crumbs and currants in the baking pan.

Place the pan in the middle of the oven and bake 15 minutes. Sprinkle the pecans on top of the pudding and bake until the pudding jiggles slightly when gently shaken, another 20 to 30 minutes.

Remove the pan from the oven and let cool on a wire rack for 10 to 20 minutes before cutting. Serve the pudding on a pool of Honey Crème Anglaise (recipe follows) or simply with a pitcher of milk or cream.

If you have leftovers, be sure to keep the pudding covered in the refrigerator for no more than 2 days.

Serves 6 to 9.

Note: We use our whole wheat French bread for this pudding. To make coarse bread crumbs, place dry bread in the bowl of a food processor and pulse several times until the bread is in about 1/4-inch pieces. Or simply cut the bread into 1/4-inch cubes.

Honey Crème Anglaise

1 1/4 cups half-and-half or whole milk
2 tablespoons honey
1/2 teaspoon arrowroot powder
1/4 cup half-and-half or whole milk
Pinch salt
1 egg yolk, beaten
1/4 teaspoon vanilla extract
1 teaspoon dark rum, optional

In a small saucepan over medium heat, scald the 1 1/4 cups half-and-half. Remove from the heat, add the honey, and stir.

Dissolve the arrowroot in the 1/4 cup half-and-half. Whisk in the salt and beaten egg yolk.

Pour half of the scalded mixture into the egg mixture, then pour it back into the pan. Over low heat, stirring slowly and constantly, cook the sauce until it has thickened slightly. Do not boil or the sauce will curdle. If this happens, you may be able to save the sauce by whisking vigorously or, as a last resort, blending briefly in an electric blender on low speed. The sauce will definitely not be as fine if you need to resort to these last methods. Keep the heat low and your attention on the sauce and you will have good results.

Remove from the heat and stir in the vanilla and rum (if used). Let the sauce cool, and then chill before serving. This tasty custard sauce is also delicious served over fresh raspberries and sliced peaches.

The sauce will keep, covered in the refrigerator, for several days.

Makes 1 1/2 cups

Apple Cobbler

▼▼▼▼▼▼▼▼▼▼▼▼▼▼▼

M mm, hot apple cobbler, one of the rewards of fall. The keys to this one are baking the apples until they are just tender, and pouring on the cake batter in one smooth motion.

Serve warm with vanilla ice cream or frozen yogurt.

2 1/2 pounds Rome, McIntosh,
or Granny Smith apples (8 cups sliced)
1/4 cup currants or raisins, optional
1 tablespoon unbleached white flour
1 1/2 teaspoons ground cinnamon
1/4 teaspoon ground nutmeg
1/3 cup apple juice
1/4 cup pure maple syrup
2 teaspoons lemon juice
1/2 teaspoon grated lemon zest
3/4 cup unsalted butter
1/2 cup pure maple syrup
1/2 teaspoon vanilla extract
1/4 cup buttermilk or 1/4 cup milk mixed
with 1 teaspoon lemon juice
1 egg, beaten
3/4 cup whole wheat pastry flour
1/2 cup unbleached white flour
1/2 teaspoon baking powder
1/8 teaspoon baking soda
1/4 teaspoon salt

Preheat the oven to 400°F

To prepare the filling, core and thinly slice the apples. Peel them only if you so desire. Place the apples in a nonreactive 9-inch square pan and top them with the currants (if used), the 1 tablespoon flour, spices, apple juice, maple syrup, lemon juice, and zest. Mix with your hands or a spoon until the apples are coated. Cover the pan with a cookie sheet and bake for 15 to 25 minutes. The apples should be slightly soft and just tender.

Meanwhile, prepare the topping. Melt the butter in a small saucepan. Remove from the heat and add the maple syrup and vanilla, which will cool the butter to room temperature. Add the buttermilk and stir. Add the egg and whisk thoroughly.

In a medium bowl measure all the dry ingredients for the topping. Add the liquid mixture and whisk only until smooth. Immediately pour the batter over the fruit in the pan. If the batter begins to thicken as you pour, pour it on in sections. Do not spread the batter to even it out.

Bake the cobbler in the top third of the oven until golden brown and firm to the touch, 25 to 35 minutes. You may wish to place a cookie sheet under the cobbler pan to catch any juicy overflow.

Remove the pan from the oven and let cool on a wire rack for 20 to 30 minutes before cutting. Serve warm.

Serves 6 to 8.

Raspberry Apple Cobbler Variation: Omit the optional currants. Top the cooked apples with 1 cup fresh raspberries, then proceed with the topping and bake as directed.

Strawberry Apple Cobbler Variation: Omit the optional currants. Decrease the lemon zest in the apple mixture to 1/4 teaspoon, and top the cooked apples with 1 cup sliced strawberries. Proceed as directed.

High-altitude instructions for 7,000 feet above sea level: Increase the buttermilk to 1/3 cup or increase the milk to 1/3 cup plus 1 1/2 teaspoons lemon juice.

Gingerbread with Lemon Sauce

▼▼▼▼▼▼▼▼▼▼▼▼▼

Gingerbread always feels so warm and nourishing as hot summer days fade into the cool crisp fall. This one is quite moist and rich. Enjoy it with hot Lemon Sauce or whipped cream.

Gingerbread

1/2 cup unsalted butter, plus butter for pan
1 1/2 teaspoons ground ginger
1 tablespoon unsweetened cocoa (see Note)
1 1/2 teaspoons ginger juice (see page 7)
1/2 cup light molasses
1/4 cup pure maple syrup
1/2 cup plain yogurt
2 eggs, beaten
1/2 cup unbleached white flour
3/4 cup whole wheat pastry flour
1 teaspoon baking powder
1/2 teaspoon baking soda
1/3 teaspoon salt
1 teaspoon ground cinnamon
1/8 teaspoon ground cloves
1/8 teaspoon ground nutmeg
1/4 cup pecans or walnuts, chopped

Preheat the oven to 350°F. Butter an 8-inch square pan and set aside.

In a small saucepan over low heat, melt the 1/2 cup butter with the ground ginger and cocoa. Add the ginger juice and remove the pan from the heat.

Add the molasses and maple syrup and let cool to lukewarm. Whisk in the yogurt and beaten eggs.

Measure the flours, baking powder, baking soda, salt, and spices into a medium bowl. Whisk the dry ingredients, then pour the liquid mixture over the dry ingredients and whisk only until smooth. Pour the batter into the buttered pan. Sprinkle the chopped nuts on top of the batter.

Bake the gingerbread in the middle of the oven until it springs back when pressed gently, 25 to 30 minutes. Remove the pan to a wire rack. If you desire to serve the cake whole on a platter, let it cool in the pan for 10 minutes, then invert the cake onto another rack. Cover the cake with the first rack and invert it again. Or you may let the cake cool completely in the pan, then cut it into squares.

Serve with Lemon Sauce (recipe follows) or cover and keep up to 1 day. Do not refrigerate.

Makes one 8-inch cake; serves 6 to 9.

Note: Any unsweetened cocoa will do nicely, but Pernigotto cocoa from Italy (sold by Williams-Sonoma) lends a silky richness to this gingerbread.

High-altitude instructions for 7,000 feet above sea level: Add 1/4 cup cool water to the beaten eggs. Decrease the baking powder to 1/4 teaspoon. Decrease the baking soda to 1/4 teaspoon.

Lemon Sauce

1/2 cup pure maple syrup
1/3 cup water
Pinch salt
2 teaspoons arrowroot dissolved
in 1/4 cup water
2 tablespoons unsalted butter
3/4 teaspoon grated lemon zest
1/3 cup lemon juice

In a small saucepan bring the maple syrup and the water to a boil. Reduce the heat to low, add the salt and dissolved arrowroot, and continue to cook until the mixture thickens and becomes translucent, stirring gently.

Add the butter, lemon zest, and lemon juice and cook only until the butter is melted. Remove from the heat.

Serve this sauce hot or at room temperature. It will keep up to several days covered in the refrigerator, but it may lose its thickness when reheated.

Makes approximately 1 cup.

Chocolate Grand Marnier Cake

▼▼▼▼▼▼▼▼▼▼▼▼▼▼

This delicious cake was inspired by my memory of a very fancy chocolate rum cake that my mother used to make for special occasions. The chocolate rum cake had fillings and frostings and, although very grand, took too much time to make very often. This cake, however, is quite elegant and simple to prepare.

Unsalted butter and flour, for pan
7 ounces unsweetened baking chocolate
3/4 cup unsalted butter
2 1/4 cups pure maple syrup
1/2 cup Grand Marnier liqueur
1 teaspoon vanilla extract
4 eggs, beaten
1 1/4 cups unbleached white flour
1/2 cup whole wheat pastry flour
1 1/2 teaspoons baking powder
1/2 teaspoon baking soda
3/4 teaspoon salt
1 teaspoon grated orange zest
1/2 teaspoon ground cardamom
1/4 cup Grand Marnier liqueur,
for brushing cooled cake

Preheat the oven to 350°F. Butter and flour a 10-inch fluted springform pan with a removable bottom. Set aside.

Melt the chocolate and butter in a small saucepan over low heat. Stir in the maple syrup, the 1/2 cup Grand Marnier, and vanilla. Let cool.

Add the beaten eggs to the completely cooled chocolate mixture.

In a large mixing bowl, measure all the dry ingredients. Add the grated orange zest and stir. Whisk the liquid mixture into the dry ingredients and mix until the batter is smooth. Pour evenly into the prepared pan. Place the pan in the middle of the oven and bake until a wooden skewer or toothpick comes out barely clean, 45 to 50 minutes. It is all right if the cake cracks on top.

Let the cake cool on a wire rack for 10 minutes before removing the outer rim of the pan. Let it cool another 5 to 10 minutes and then invert the cake onto the rack.

When the cake has cooled completely, brush with the 1/4 cup Grand Marnier. If not serving immediately, cover the cake with plastic wrap. It will keep very well for 1 day. Do not refrigerate.

Makes one 10-inch cake; serves 12.

<u>Chocolate Rum Cake Variation:</u> Omit the orange zest and cardamom, and substitute dark rum for the Grand Marnier, both in the cake and for brushing later.

<u>High-altitude instructions for 7,000 feet above sea level:</u> Decrease the baking powder to 1 1/4 teaspoons. Decrease the baking soda to 1/4 teaspoon. Bake 50 to 55 minutes.

Coconut Cake
with Mango Orange Sauce

▼▼▼▼▼▼▼▼▼▼▼▼▼▼

Coconut is not in fashion these days because of worries about saturated fat. However, it is a marvelous fruit, and a little goes a long way. This cake is a delicate summer extravagance paired with our Mango Orange Sauce.

Coconut Cake

Unsalted butter and flour, for pan
1/2 cup unsalted butter
1/2 cup plus 2 tablespoons pure maple syrup
1/3 cup half-and-half or whole milk
1/2 teaspoon vanilla extract
1 1/2 teaspoons lemon juice
1/4 teaspoon lemon zest
2 eggs, beaten
3/4 cup unbleached white flour
1/2 cup whole wheat pastry flour
1 teaspoon baking powder
1/4 teaspoon baking soda
1/4 teaspoon salt
1/4 teaspoon ground cardamom
1/2 cup unsweetened shredded coconut
2 tablespoons unsweetened shredded coconut,
for topping cake

Preheat the oven to 350°F. Butter and flour an 8-inch square pan. Set aside. Melt the 1/2 cup butter in a small saucepan over low heat. Remove from the heat and add the maple syrup, half-and-half, vanilla, and lemon juice. When the mixture has cooled to lukewarm, add the lemon zest and whisk in the beaten eggs.

In a large bowl whisk together the liquid mixture and dry ingredients and whisk until the batter is smooth. Pour evenly into the prepared pan. Sprinkle the 2 tablespoons coconut on top of the batter.

Place the pan in the center of the oven and bake until golden or until a wooden skewer or toothpick comes out clean, 25 to 30 minutes. Remove the pan to a wire rack. If you desire to serve the cake whole on a platter, let it cool in the pan for about 10 minutes, then invert the cake onto another rack. Cover the cake with the first rack and invert it again. Or you may let the cake cool completely in the pan, then cut it into squares.

Serve with Mango Orange Sauce (recipe follows) or cover and keep up to 1 day. Do not refrigerate.

Makes one 8-inch cake; serves 6 to 9.

High-altitude instructions for 7,000 feet above sea level: Increase the half-and-half to 1/3 cup plus 1 tablespoon. Decrease the baking powder to 3/4 teaspoon.

Mango Orange Sauce

1/2 cup pure maple syrup
1 1/2 teaspoons grated orange zest
1 tablespoon arrowroot powder
1/4 cup water
1/2 cup orange juice
1 tablespoon lemon juice
1 ripe mango, pitted, peeled,
and diced into 1/4-inch cubes

In a small nonreactive saucepan, simmer the maple syrup and orange zest for 3 minutes.

Dissolve the arrowroot in the water. Add to the maple syrup mixture and bring to a boil, stirring constantly with a wooden spoon. When the sauce thickens and clears remove from the heat immediately.

Add the orange juice and lemon juice. Strain through a fine sieve and let cool completely.

Stir the diced mango into the sauce. Serve immediately for best flavor and texture.

Makes 1 1/2 cups.

Almond Crumb Pie Crust

▼▼▼▼▼▼▼▼▼▼▼▼▼▼

This easy and versatile crust has a light, nutty flavor that is compatible with many fillings.

1 cup plus 2 tablespoons whole wheat pastry flour
3/4 teaspoon ground cinnamon
1/4 cup almonds, ground
Pinch salt
1/4 cup corn oil or canola oil
1 tablespoon barley malt syrup,
or sorghum syrup (see Note)
1 1/2 teaspoons pure maple syrup

In a small bowl mix together the flour, cinnamon, ground almonds, and salt.

Mix together the oil, barley malt, and maple syrup and pour over the dry ingredients. Blend with a fork. Press into an oiled pie pan, making sure that you leave no holes.

This crust freezes well before it is baked.

Makes one 9-inch crust.

Note: Barley malt syrup and sorghum syrup are available in natural foods stores.

Pecan Crumb Pie Crust Variation: Substitute 1/4 cup pecans for the almonds. Decrease the oil by 1 tablespoon.

Maple Pecan Pie

▼▼▼▼▼▼▼▼▼▼▼▼▼▼

Pecan pie is one of those intensely sweet treats that actually needs whipped cream or vanilla ice cream to "lighten" it. This one takes advantage of the wonderful flavor combination of maple syrup and pecans.

1 Pecan Crumb Pie Crust (see page 108)
2 1/2 cups pecan halves
1 cup pure maple syrup
1/4 cup barley malt syrup,
or sorghum syrup (see Note)
1/4 cup unsalted butter
3 eggs, beaten
1/8 teaspoon salt
1 teaspoon vanilla extract

Prepare the crumb crust and bake in a 400°F oven until barely golden brown, 5 to 7 minutes. Let the crust cool on a wire rack before filling.

Reduce the oven temperature to 325°F. Roast the pecans in a dry pan until they are fragrant but not browned, 5 to 8 minutes. Let the pecans cool thoroughly.

In a small saucepan over medium heat, bring the maple syrup and barley malt to a boil. Reduce the heat and simmer for 2 to 3 minutes. Add the butter and continue cooking only until it is melted. Remove from the heat.

In a medium bowl whisk together the beaten eggs, salt, and vanilla. Whisking constantly, slowly add the hot syrup to the egg mixture. Stir in the toasted pecans. Pour the filling into the cooled crust and bake until the filling is barely firm, 35 to 40 minutes. Let the pie cool on a wire rack. Serve at room temperature. This pie may be covered and refrigerated for 1 day.

Makes one 9-inch pie; serves 8.

Note: Barley malt syrup and sorghum syrup are available in natural foods stores.

Judy's Pumpkin Pie

▼▼▼▼▼▼▼▼▼▼▼▼▼

This is a traditional pumpkin pie. Judy Knapp has refined this recipe so that her mouth waters every time she makes it.

One 3-pound sugar pie pumpkin,
or 2 cups canned pumpkin puree
1 Almond Crumb Pie Crust,
or Pecan Crumb Pie Crust (see page 108)
1 egg yolk mixed with 1 teaspoon water
2/3 cup pure maple syrup
1 tablespoon light molasses
3/4 cup whipping cream
2 eggs, beaten
1/2 teaspoon salt
1 1/2 teaspoons ground cinnamon
1/2 teaspoon ground nutmeg
1/2 teaspoon ground ginger
1/8 teaspoon ground cloves
1/8 teaspoon black pepper
2 teaspoons unbleached white flour
1/2 teaspoon vanilla extract
2 teaspoons dark rum, optional

Preheat the oven to 375°F. Pierce the skin of the pumpkin and place it in a dry pan. Bake the pumpkin until the flesh feels soft when pierced with a bamboo skewer or knife, approximately 45 minutes. Cut the pumpkin in half to cool. Scrape out the seeds and carefully scoop out the cooked pumpkin. Purée the pumpkin in a food processor or blender. Or you may mash the pumpkin thoroughly by hand. Be careful not to include any of the pumpkin skin in the pie. Measure the amount needed for the pie and refrigerate any remaining pumpkin purée for another use.

Meanwhile, increase the oven temperature to 400°F and bake the prepared crust on the lowest rack until barely golden brown, 5 to 7 minutes. Brush the crust with the egg and water mixture and return to the oven for 1 minute. Let the crust cool completely on a wire rack.

Reduce the oven temperature to 350°F. In a medium bowl, mix together the cooled pumpkin purée and all the other ingredients. Whisk this filling until smooth. Pour the pumpkin filling into the pie crust and bake in the lower third of the oven until the center of the pie is nearly firm when gently jiggled, 50 to 60 minutes.

Remove the pie to a wire rack to cool. It tastes best served at room temperature with a dollop of whipped cream or vanilla ice cream.

If necessary, the pie may be refrigerated, covered when completely cold, and held for 1 day.

Makes one 9-inch pie; serves 8.

Lemon Custard Pie

▼▼▼▼▼▼▼▼▼▼▼▼▼

*E*njoy this delicious dessert on a hot summer day. Serve as is or dress it up with fresh berries and whipped cream. Please eat the pie the day it is made, since the crust will not keep well.

1 Almond Crumb Pie Crust (see page 108)
1 egg yolk mixed with 1 teaspoon water
2 1/4 cups sour cream
1 teaspoon unbleached white flour
1/3 cup honey
3 egg yolks, beaten
2 whole eggs, beaten
1/8 teaspoon salt
2 teaspoons grated lemon zest
1/4 cup plus 1 tablespoon lemon juice
1 teaspoon lime juice
1 teaspoon grated lemon zest, for garnish

Bake the crust on the lowest rack of a 400°F oven until barely golden brown, 5 to 7 minutes. Brush the crust with the egg and water and return it to the oven for 1 minute. Let the crust cool completely on a wire rack before proceeding.

Reduce the oven temperature to 300°F. Whisk together the sour cream, flour, and honey. Add the beaten egg yolks and whole eggs and mix well. Add the salt, the 2 teaspoons lemon zest, and the lemon and lime juices. Whisk together until smooth.

Pour this filling into the partially baked and cooled crust and garnish with the 1 teaspoon lemon zest. Bake the pie in the bottom third of the oven until the filling appears nearly firm when gently jiggled, 45 to 55 minutes. The pie will continue to set as it cools.

Remove the pie to a wire rack to cool. When completely cool, refrigerate the pie until serving. Cover the pie after it has chilled. If you cover it earlier, condensation will form as it cools, and the crust will become soggy.

Makes one 9-inch pie; serves 8.

Fudge Pecan Pie

▼▼▼▼▼▼▼▼▼▼▼▼▼

In Santa Fe, restaurants come and go with the breeze. The inspiration for this recipe came from eating at a short-lived Cajun restaurant and being very impressed by a chocolate pecan pie.

1 Pecan Crumb Pie Crust (see page 108)
2 1/2 cups pecan halves
1 ounce unsweetened baking chocolate
1/3 cup unsalted butter
1 cup pure maple syrup
1/2 cup cocoa powder
2 teaspoons unbleached white flour
1/4 teaspoon salt
1 teaspoon vanilla extract
2 tablespoons whipping cream
3 eggs, beaten

Bake the crust on the lowest rack of a 400°F oven until barely golden brown, 5 to 7 minutes. Let the crust cool on a wire rack.

Reduce the oven temperature to 325°F. Roast the pecans in a dry pan until they are fragrant but not browned, 5 to 8 minutes. Let the pecans cool completely.

In a small saucepan over low heat, melt the chocolate and butter. Remove the pan from the heat and add the maple syrup.

Measure the cocoa, flour, and salt into a medium bowl. Whisk in the chocolate mixture. Add the vanilla, whipping cream, and beaten eggs and whisk until smooth. Stir in the cooled pecans.

Pour the filling into the partially baked crust and bake in the bottom third of the oven until the center of the pie is nearly firm, approximately 30 minutes. Let the pie cool on a wire rack, then chill briefly. Serve topped with whipped cream or vanilla ice cream.

The pie will keep well for 1 day, covered in the refrigerator.

Makes one 9-inch pie; serves 8 to 10.

Selected Bibliography

Alford, Jeffrey & Duguid, Naomi. _Seductions of Rice_. New York: Artisan, 1998.

Berenbaum, Rose Levy. _The Cake Bible_. New York: William Morrow and Company, Inc., 1988.

Bertolli, Paul with Alice Waters. _Chez Panisse Cooking_. New York: Random House, 1988.

Bianchini, Francesco. _The Complete Book of Fruits & Vegetables_. New York: Crown Publishers, Inc. 1973.

Chung, Henry. _Henry Chung's Hunan Style Chinese Cookbook_. New York: Crown Publishers, 1978.

Creasy, Rosalind. _Cooking From The Garden_. San Francisco: Sierra Club Books, Inc., 1986

Davidson, Alan. _The Oxford Companion To Food_. New York: Oxford University Press, Inc., 1999.

Devi, Yamuna. _Lord Krishna's Cuisine_. Old Westbury, NY: Bala Books, 1987.

Dowwel, Philip, & Baily, Adrian. _Cook's Ingredients_. New York: William Morrow & Co., 1980.

Gelb, Barbara Levine. _The Dictionary of Food_. London: Paddington Press, 1978.

Haedrich, Ken. _The Maple Syrup Cookbook_. Pownal, Vt.: Garden Way Publishing, 1989.

Herbst, Sharon Tyler. _Food Lover's Companion_. New York: Barron's Educational Series, Inc., 1990

Hillman, Howard. _The Cook's Book_. New York: Avon Books, 1981.

Jaffrey, Madhur. _An Invitation to Indian Cooking_. New York: Bantam Books, 1975.

Kennedy, Diana. _The Art of Mexican Cooking_. New York: Bantam Books, 1989.

Machlin, Edda Servi. _The Classic Cuisine of The Italian Jews_. New York: Dodd, Mead & Co., 1981.

Madison, Deborah. _Vegetarian Cooking for Everyone_. New York: Broadway Books, 1997.

Robertson, Laurel, Carol Flinders, and Bronwen Godfrey. _The New Laurel's Kitchen_, 2nd. ed. Berkeley: Ten Speed Press, 1986.

Rombauer, Irma S., Rombauer, Marion, and Becker, Ethan. _All New All Purpose Joy of Cooking_ by New York: Scribner, 1997.

Root, Waverly. _Food_. New York: Simon & Schuster Publishing, 1980.

Sahni, Julie. _Classic Indian Vegetarian and Grain Cooking_. New York: William Morrow and Company, Inc., 1985.

Weaver, William Woys. _Heirloom Vegetable Gardening_. New York: Henry Holt and Co., 1997.

Wolcott, Imogene. _The New England Yankee Cook Book_. New York: Coward-McCann, Inc., 1939.

Yoneda, Soei. _Good Food from a Japanese Temple_. Tokyo: Kodansha International, 1982.

Yee, Rhoda. _Chinese Village Cookbook_. San Francisco: Yerba Press, 1975.

Index